AF413416

Colophon
Set Margins' #78

H oming
I n,
S haring
K nowledge:

Essays, Conversations, and Notes on HISK laureates, 2016-23

John C. Welchman

ISBN: 978-90-835325-2-3

Editor: John C. Welchman
Graphic design: Freek Lomme
Text editor: John C. Welchman
Proofreader: Aaron Bogart
Artists: Femmy Otten, Chloé Op de Beeck, Lisa Wilkens, Ariane Loze, buren, Vesna Faassen & Lukas Verdijk, Adja Yunkers and Indrikis Gelzis, Katya Ev, Sofia Caesar, Nikolay Karabinovych, Helen Anna Flanagan, Nelleke Cloosterman, and Danielle Kaganov.
Fonts: Blacker Mono book and Calvino Thin by Zetafonts

Made possible thanks to the generous donation of time and resource by John C. Welchman and Freek Lomme; and the support of the artist and of HISK, which facilitated the initial conversations and many of the writings.

first print, 2025

www.setmargins.press

Homing
I
S
Knowledge

Preface

John C. Welchman

> A dialogue that in real life is a source of delight, when turned into writing and read, is a picture with nothing but false perspectives. Everything is too long or too short.
>
> &&&
>
> During a long talk the wisest of men becomes a fool once and a simpleton thrice.
>
> — Friedrich Nietzsche, *Human All-Too-Human: A Book for Free Spirits*, Part II (1880)[1]

In March 2022 the 'managing agreement' for the artist residency program HISK (Hoger Instituut voor Schone Kunsten; Higher Institute for Fine Arts Advanced Studies & Practice-Based Research in Visual Arts) was not renewed by the Flemish government. As a result, the cycle of two-year residencies sadly came to an end with the last participants graduating in December 2023. This is not the place to investigate or pronounce on the relatively complex and sometimes convoluted series of events that transpired at the end of HISK's quarter of a century of peration, or on follow-up efforts to re-establish HISK in another form.

The purpose of this small volume is, rather, to offer what is effectively a personal testimony to the creativity and vitality of the quite extraordinary range of Flemish and international artists who benefited from the signature opportunity to work for a couple of years in the generously proportioned studio spaces of HISK, located from its inception in 1997 in Antwerp; then for some decade and a half in the Leopold Barracks in Ghent; and finally, for the program's last couple of years, in the Gosset building in Molenbeek-Saint-Jean, Brussels.

I was one of a shifting roster of Belgian and international artists,curators, critics, art and media historians (and others) who were invited to HISK in order to make individual studio visits, sometimes to offer lectures or seminars, and, more occasionally, to join program participants in one or another of the exhibition or location visits that were organized to benefit them. The regimen was often exacting. On a visiting day I would arrive at the HISK office in the morning for a quick cup of coffee and a welcoming chat, and be presented with a schedule that would typically involve back-to-back studio visits of one hour each, but sometimes of an hour and a-half (when the meeting was a first-time encounter or with a media artist who wanted to show a finished work or work in progress). There was a break for a picnic-style salad lunch in the middle of the day, when visitors would sit down for an hour or so with the HISK staff, including the director or curator when possible, and sometimes with a few of the artists. The afternoon visits would be scheduled through about 5:00 or 6:00 pm; but one of the inevitabilities of the setup was an overhang at the end of the day as the timetable was recalibrated, conversations rounded out, and our ex-changes went into extra time.

The normal protocol at HISK was for a small group of visiting artists and lecturers to convene on the same couple of days, so that visits were predictable and rhythmic. In this format, one evening during the visit would be programmed so that each visitor could give brief remarks on their work or research in progress. Because I live in Los Angeles and teach at the University of California, it was harder for me to coordinate precisely with these designated schedules. So, I would typically visit during a trip to Europe that included other research, curatorial projects, or lectures. I was also granted leeway with the reporting procedure, so that instead of drawing up notes on each meeting, as was customary, artists were asked to follow up with any questions or comments that had arisen from our exchanges; and I would respond.

The studio visit, or 'crit,' is of course a staple of art school curricula and residency etiquette. As a genre of commissioned exchange, it has often been over- and under-thought—the former situation producing a probationary web of permissibilities, taboos, constraints, and infringements, the latter promoting a loose *laissez-faire* that sometimes equates anything goes with a recoil from the power and identitarian dynamics that accompany any social interaction, but particularly those that are organized and contracted. The exchange depends, somewhat uncannily, on the capacities of the critter and critee. On the one hand, openness, honesty, candor, the ability to listen and to shape and frame questions as well as what may be seen and heard as judgment-type commentary. On the other, the choice of what to present and how; and of the kind and extent of the contexts (historical, biographical, philosophical) that preface or accompany a showing. One could meditate for pages or hours on these quite simple parameters; but there's little point because the heterogeneity of encounters and conversations—how they start and wind, flow and unravel—immediately and cumulatively color and contour any exchange, even when its progression is beset by purpose or would-be self-conscious mediation.

Getting ahold of any of this is a bit like the problem with the discourse of aesthetics: can we really believe in generalities that might embrace the formats, qualities, propositions, pleasures, historicity, or disturbances intrinsic to the generalized category of 'artwork?' But more so, because a conversation or meeting is above all else a moment of social becoming. It is meted out by off-stage causes and effects, by happenstance, and by a to-and-fro that can be performative and impromptu, creative or reductive, cumulative or regressive. Its momentum might be advanced or interrupted by so many variables that are seldom explicitly reckoned with—behavioral and circumstantial anomalies, awkward silences, breathless run-ons, and a vast palette of misunderstandings and disconnects. Or—most likely, and—it might be seasoned with rapport, creative intuition, moments of genuine insight, dialogical 'progress,' or, occasionally, revelation. Many visits are tangled up in several of these, and other, possibilities—a conversation that seemed to be going nowhere suddenly fires up (or the other way around). In any event, you become accustomed to switching over to what meets the moment.

HISK participants were selected by a committee of artists, critics, and curators, often including noted alumni, generally chaired by the director, later the curator, of the program. For most of my some decade and a half of visits an interesting mix of nationalities, genres, and practice orientations emerged from the jury process—as reflected in this volume, which includes discussions with or about the work of artists from Belgium, Netherlands, Ukraine, UK, Israel, Russia, Brazil, and Latvia—most of whom had lived in one or more other locations. The visiting routine at HISK could be intense, even overwhelming. As I was preparing this volume, one contributor, who had arrived as the youngest member of their cohort, shared that they felt almost besieged in the first year by perhaps fifty visitors, each giving advice, or making suggestions and comments that were different, sometimes antithetical. As some artists (understandably) took fewer meetings and others were traveling for exhibitions or research, and because I was in Belgium, typically, for just a few days a year, who I visited and whether or not they had current or recent work in their studio (or were motivated to discuss it) was in the lap of the gods. The texts that follow are not, therefore, anything like a 'curated' selection in which I made active choices or inclusions; they simply represent meetings with thirteen artists that for one reason or another gave rise to writing by mutual agreement. Of course, both parties in a sense 'wanted' or were open to a more formalized collaboration, but I think it's fair to say that in most cases neither planned for it from the get-go.

It follows, in a related dimension, that the texts offer a snapshot of the density of my work at HISK, centered on a sequence of five of more collaborations around 2017 with another burst of activity during the last couple of years of HISK's recent life (2020-23). Building on earlier research on René Magritte and Surrealism, by 2017 I had developed, or was about to, a series of books and catalogue essays on Belgium-based artists, including Cuban-born Ricardo Brey, Guillaume Bijl (Brey and Bijl were regular lecturers at HISK), Koen van den Broek (a HISK alumnus), and, most recently, Marcel Broodthaers.[2] Several of these projects were developed over the years alongside or around visits to HISK, inflecting my own program of research and writing quite substantially.

From my earliest visits beginning around 2008, I would generally offer an evening lecture for the current participants, alumni (known as 'laureates'), HISK friends, and a wider public. These events were normally programmed in the HISK lecture spaces, but we occasionally partnered with local museums or academies, including SMAK (Stedelijk Museum voor Actuele Kunst or Municipal Museum of Contemporary Art), located in the nearby Citadelpark, WIELS Centre for Contemporary Art in Brussels, and KASK (Koninklijke Academie voor Schone Kunsten van Gent or Royal Academy of Fine Arts). Sharing research outcomes and works in progress was, for me, and–judging by comments and feedback from HISK laureates–for some others at least, a key part of my relationship with and contribution to HISK. A good number of studio conversations and subsequent email exchanges drilled down into or departed from something ventured in the talk presented the previous evening. And discussions were framed as much, I think, by way of creative disagreements, different takes and points of view, or provisos, as through the navigation of a common understanding or approach. It's hard, probably impossible, to represent this aspect of my work at HISK, but here's a (partial) list of talks and topics shared at HISK or partner venues over the last decade and a half.

'Paul McCarthy and the Piratic' (2008)
'The Art of Mike Kelley (Soup to Nuts)' (2014)
'Past Realization' (talk and book launch, WIELS, 2016)
'Guillaume Bijl' (KASK, 2017)
'The Work of Femmy Otten' (talk and book launch, 2017)
'Gift Vouchers: Giving and Rebates in the Age of Appropriation' (2019)
'Art and Writing' (2019)
'Tala Madani: Shit Moms' (remote, 2020)

‘Faces and Powers’ (2021)
‘The Uncanny and Visual Culture’ (2022)
‘Meltdown: Constituencies of Disappearance (in the work of Mike Kelley)’ (Herbert Foundation, Ghent, 2023)
‘On the Politics of Video Installation: Yoshua Okon’ (L,Académie royale des Beaux-Arts, École supérieure des Arts, Brussels, 2023)
‘Royal Book Lodge’ (talk and book launch, KIN, Brussels, 2023)

While generating talking points and debate, the lecture program and studio visits didn't overlap much, topically or conceptually–with a couple of exceptions, one briefly visible in the following pages. In 2016 I was invited to present a keynote lecture at the international conference ‘Global Adorno’ programmed by University of Amsterdam, which gave rise to an illustrated talk, ‘Search for a Symbol’ (March 21, 2016).[3] The research and writing of the lecture and the development for publication of an associated essay in 2016–17[4] coincided with efforts at HISK to produce seminars or discussion groups based on the writings of various theorists and philosophers, including Adorno, and with my own teaching at UCSD, which had given rise to a graduate course on Adorno's *Aesthetic Theory* in winter 2015. As questions arising were, then, on my mind at this time as well as in discussion among HISKers, it's not surprising that they surface in the two most informal texts in the anthology: the email exchanges with Chloé Op de Beeck and Lisa Wilkens, both generated in Spring 2017.

0

The studio visit is the diffuse legatee of a signal shift in Western thinking about the nature and purpose of conversation–that ‘most fruitful and natural exercise of the mind’ as Michel de Montaigne famously put it.[5] In an arc of reflections that reaches from Montaigne to eighteenth-century essayists including Joseph Addison, Richard Steele, and Samuel Johnson, the exchange of frank and robust dialogue between peers was conceived of in relation to, and at the service of, a salutary spectrum of affirmative characteristics includng self-fashioning (and -correction) and performative, socially grounded civility, and, sometimes at least, epistemological surprise. But there is a turn that reroutes aspects of this tradition at the onset of what we might term professionalized modernity. We see its shape emerge in Hegel's Preface to *Phenomenology of Spirit* where he points to what he constructs as a legacy of conversational exchange that offers a ‘kind of knowing and judging [that] will still retain its appropriate place in ordinary conversation.' But the ordinary or everyday is not enough here to account for the implications of 'culture and its laborious emergence from the immediacy of substantial life'; and it is especially insufficient to reckon with Hegel's formulation of the need for a new kind of philosophical inquiry in the unfolding of which 'the real issue has been penetrated to its depths by serious speculative effort.'[6] Later in the 'Preface' Hegel doubles down on what he terms the 'looser form' of 'method . . . more blended with the arbitrary and the accidental' associated with 'conversation.' For 'once the necessity of the Notion (*Begriff*) has banished the slipshod style of conversational discussion, and along with it the pedantry and pomposity of science, they are not to be replaced by the non-method of presentiment and inspiration, or by the arbitrariness of prophetic utterance, both of which despise not only scientific pomposity, but scientific procedure of all kinds.'[7] What replaces conversation—but also prophesy and science—methodologically, is the dialectic, a studied mode of argumentative progression that trawls the depths and engenders the movements of properly philosophical thinking and concept production.

The eclipse of conversation—in this case by the inexorable sculpting force of the dialectic and its often mysterious pathways to truth—will be replayed in any number of modern categories that override the knowledge production of informal exchange, including *structure* and *form*, on the one hand, and the precedence ascribed to moral or ethical imperatives on the other. Several artists, critics, and movements in the twentieth century put illuminating pressure on these constructs. During the last year of World War I, Richard Huelsenbeck, for example, insisted that a Dada orientation, capacity or 'state of mind' could be 'revealed in any conversation whatever' in which one 'let oneself be thrown by things.'[8] Conversation, masquerading as old-order revelation, is, here, the guarantor of the improvised disordering that allows a Dada disposition to be known. For Naum Gabo and Anton Pevsner, writing in a public poster-form a couple of years later in summer 1920, the very future of engaged modes of practice was predicated on a shared assumption that '[a]rt is no mere ground for conversation but the source of real exaltation, our word and deed.' The distanced, perhaps artificial, construct of the conversation is, here, taken over by something surpassing, an 'exaltation' imbued—like conversation—with language-derived purpose ('words') but that is also manifest as an action or 'deed.'[9]

In the neo-avant-garde disquisitions of the 1960s, the relation between art and conversation was colored by ghosted replays of both inclusiveness and absurdity—as in the accretive, everyday run-on of Claes Oldenburg's manifesto originally composed for the catalogue of the exhibition *Environments, Situations and Spaces* at Martha Jackson

Gallery (May–June, 1961), where he writes: 'I am for the art of conversation between the sidewalk and a blind man's metal stick.' Here the space of spoken exchange is displaced by a differently predicated capacity to navigate by touch and feel—as the exchange of words is replaced by the paralinguistic tap of a cane—and the privileged sightfulness of an artwork upended by another form of insight in which both vision and language are absent. A decade later, facing expulsion from the Kunstakademie in Düsseldorf, where he served as Professor of Sculpture from 1961 to 1972, Joseph Beuys rounds on the individualized declensions of two-party exchange, noting that—in situations where a lot is at stake—while 'things start with answers to questions' he has turned away from 'private conversations.' Scenes of individual discussion are not as 'effective,' he contends, as group exchange in 'large classes' in which 'everyone can learn something from every correction. That way each student learns from others' problems as well as his [sic] own.' The 'public discussion' for which Beuys advocates is explicitly connected to a mode of 'group therapy' in which 'people should put their private hang-ups into words.' It is underwritten by a concept of the school or academy that dispenses with 'fixed teaching plan[s],' specific 'work places' and all forms of curricular predisposition. Instead, the school itself should be reconfigured as a 'meeting place,' a non-hierarchical space for a kind of interrogatory performance. When pushed, the therapeutic impulse that informs Beuys's thinking runs into a contentious endgame as he reflects that the new form of academy is 'sometimes . . . really like a special school for the handicapped, developing the most primitive forms.'

Oldenburg's 'blind man' and Beuys's 'school for the handicapped' not only italicize the ableist assumptions of the 'special' conditions in which art might emerge, but also reveal the often covert 'corrective' assumptions about how conversation has the capacity to cure, or as Beuys puts it, to 'clear things up.'[10]

The diagnostic arena in which Beuys situated the psychodynamics of a putatively therapeutic school were not lost on the more skeptical discussants of the mode of exchange between art and conversation. In a letter addressed to the curator of a 1982 exhibition of their work in Vancouver, Canada, Art & Language (here Michael Baldwin, Mel Ramsden, and Charles Harrison) pointed to the 'psychiatric syndrome' of hysteria, suggesting that 'people are reduced to it when the idioms of conversation fail.' If Beuys expanded the scope of conversation from an individual exchange to the mass of an academy, Art & Language posit a wider envelope still—implicating nothing less, in fact, than the framework of the art world itself: 'In art's, first world,' they contend, 'conversation has failed in a collapse of differential semantics.' To propagate this dystopian regimen the management and structuring of promotion by 'critics, curators and middle-men' is transacted in an imperialist-type 'domain of legitimation'—predicated on the 'neglect' of 'method, explanation' and more properly adjudicated 'causal determinations.' With characteristic rhetorical surplus, what results, they announce, is a 'parapractical obloquy' that undermines anything 'serious' (perhaps that 'serious speculative effort' in the Hegelian sense) or 'historically vivid'—leaving only a 'masque or travesty of the indolent and fraudulent' ventured in 'a debacle of fugitive and often demented themes' and nurtured only by 'double meaning, displacement, irony, mendacity, absurdity.'[11]

∞

If studio meetings and public lectures focused most of my time at HISK, during the later years of my visits I organized a series of writing workshops, based on a similar program I had developed at the Rijksakademie van beeldende kunsten in Amsterdam, where I also served as an Advisor for a decade or so. The half-day sessions with five or six participants were purposed to assist artists who had or were developing a writing practice in English. They were open to any genre—critical or theoretical, fiction, poetry, scripting, interviews, epistolary, diaristic, and any modes of textual experimentation—with the exception of grant-writing and business or commercial exchange. A week to ten days before the meeting, each participant would share writings with each workshop attendee, generally from ten to fifteen pages; which everyone undertook to read carefully, annotating or taking notes. The first part of the workshop developed from a frank and carefully framed conversation about the stakes and responsibilities, pitfalls and pleasures of interpersonal critical exchange, responding to questions and concerns arising about caring, candor, and confidence. I found that the more honest, engaged, and intense this grounding, the better the workshop was able to dig deep into writing processes, techniques, and assumptions by interrogating and challenging but not undermining or disrespecting the work that had been shared. Even though I often circulated a (much modified) questionnaire addressing the thorniest issues in writing-directed group dynamics, there was, of course, no formula for this preamble, as each workshop needed to find its own voice, spacing, empathy, and critical spark. When everyone felt able to move on, the remainder of the session was dedicated to close consideration of the submitted writings, with all participants allocated the same amount of time, and everyone given space to share reflections on each tabled text.

The writing workshops gave rise to some of the most fulfilling moments of my work at HISK. Their dialogical unfolding, predicated on the shared stakes of sharing, would often fire up into surprising, occasionally unsettling, text-facing experiences—as participants confronted habits, assumptions, creative adaptations, aporia, tropic exigencies, and many other language-oriented (but also socially embedded) effects about which they may not have been aware before the exchange. Readings and understandings emerged, often carefully established, that no one else had been able to see or hear. Like my lectures—more so, perhaps—the workshops are difficult to 'represent.' But they stand in for a kind of middle ground in the meeting regimen, situated between the complex and unpredictable one-on-one conversations of studio visits and the more conventional at-a-distance setup of the institution-wide or public lecture. In the end, it was the shifting focal range of these (loosely speaking) pedagogical engagements (close-up; middle distance; podium remote) and their differentially embodied participant or audience clusters (1 – 5 – 50) that allowed for a fuller range of mentoring, sharing and mutual learning.

000

The essays that follow are tied, root and branch, to conversations, explorations and discoveries transacted over the years in the studios at HISK. Half or more—those on Ariane Loze, buren, Vesna Faassen & Lukas Verdijk, Sofia Caesar, Helen Anna Flanagan, Nelleke Cloosterman, and Danielle Kaganov—were occasioned by a standard protocol at HISK according to which participants roughly halfway through their second and final year nominated one of the visiting lecturers to write a brief text on the body of work they intended to present at the end-of-year exhibition in the fall or winter, which would appear in the associated catalogue. As I saw it, the task in these cases was to pay

careful critical attention to the work itself, sometimes
unfinished when the text was composed, but at the same
to open it up and situate it in relation to one or another of a hopefully well-adjudicated set of wider issues
and contexts. A measure of the importance of close discussion in front of a work-in-progress is furnished in
the email exchange with Lisa Wilkens—which did not, in
this case, lead to a catalogue essay—where the artist
refers to a difficult situation: absent a close encounter, the critic brought in by an exhibiting gallery
might have mis- or under-read the work in discussion.
This disjunction gave rise to an artist-generated 'count-
er-text,' reproduced at the end of chapter 3.

Most of the HISK exhibition essays emerged through a
combination of—usually several—engaged in situ discussions and follow-up interviews and emails, the impromptu
and run-on tenor of the former meshing with the more de-
liberated possibilities of a written exchange. The texts
home in on a work, series, or installation recently finished or in progress, usually taking off from what
seemed to me the leading issue or debate that arose in
conversation, thus building on a knowledge base that was
co-emergent between artist and visitor. I would then develop and consolidate my reflections from this point of
departure, with a view to creating a response, and fur-
nishing a focused critical framework for the exhibited
work.

The brevity of many of the essays—the shortest (on
Ariane Loze) is only five hundred, others around a
thousand, words—mitigates against anything that's in any
way comprehensive or that drills down effectively into
the critical, historical, or other contexts that might
ground the work. They are simply responses, quite immediate and direct, to the call of the practice as encountered and circumnavigated by studio conversation. The
slightly longer exhibition essays on Nikolay Karabinovych, Helen Anna Flanagan, and Danielle Kaganov manage
to push a little bit further, so that some of the key

investigations taken on in each body of work—notions of witnessing and testifying (Karabinovych), 'mediality' (Flanagan), and what I describe as 'visualized fantasies of violence, sexuality, irony, and submission' (Kaganov)—are sketched out as critical preliminaries.

A few essays have commissioning contexts outside of HISK. The first and longest chapter was written for a book on Dutch artist Femmy Otten, who was later in residence at the Rijksakademie in Amsterdam, where we also had studio visits. My aim here was to offer an overview of Otten's early career (up to 2015-16) with a view to investigating what I termed her 'partitive aesthetics'—articulated by 'fractures and cuts . . . predicated on psychological or cultural splits often articulated by hybrid and discontinuous forms.' I organized one of the key manifestations of Otten's refracted vision by way of her navigation between various historical moments emblematized by a range of defining artworks: 478-74 BCE: *The Charioteer of Delphi* (*Heniokhos [Ηνίοχος]*, the rein-holder); First Half of the Twelfth Century and Later: Figures and Heads at Angkor Wat; 1435-40: Rogier van der Weyden, *Portrait of a Young Women* (or *Lady Wearing a Gauze Headdress*); After 1457: Piero della Francesca, *Madonna del Parto*; Circa 1450-1550: German Limewood Sculpture; 1986: Andrei Tarkovsky, *Sculpting in Time*.

The essay on Katya Ev took off from an 'infiltrated performance' *Le Plus Objet des Objets* (2019) curated for the performance program by Azad Asifovich and Noëlle Chabert at Musée Zadkine, Paris, France, on the occasion of the exhibition *L'Instinct de la Matière*. It was first published in online form in *From Scratch to Scratch*, KASK Curatorial Studies, Ghent, Belgium, 2020. 'Lucidity Is Rage: Adja Yunkers and Indrikis Gelzis' was commissioned by the Belenius Gallery, Stockholm, Sweden, for the catalogue of the two-person exhibition *The Man in the Moon: Adja Yunkers and Indrikis Gelzis* (February 22 to April 1, 2018), and is the only essay in this volume (with the exception of the first chapter, which is organized around art-predicated intertexts) that puts the work of a HISK artist into relation with another body of practice, in this case paintings and collages by the noted eastern European artist Adja Yunkers (b. Riga, 1900, d. New York, 1983) from the 1920s through the 1970s.

Apart from the two email exchanges, which offer a different form of communing, there is only one example in the following pages of the dialogical genre of a conversation, which, on reflection, might be best suited to the kinds and textures of exchange in which I participated at HISK. This is the discussion 'Maintenance and Breakdown' with Sofia Caesar, who grew up in Rio de Janeiro, Brazil, which we taped one afternoon in her HISK studio surrounded by some of the objects and installations that she would present in the final group exhibition at HISK later in 2019. Our somewhat sprawling discussion was reduced and re-sequenced for publication–to respect the number of pages allocated to each participant–a formatting that was functional and effective. We returned to the original transcript here and present the conversation in its longer, original form–which gives a better sense of the twists and turns of our thinking and how each voice responds and calls to the other.[12]

Before signing off I want to offer my thanks and deep appreciation to Isabel Devriendt, who was the coordinator–and animator–of most of my visits to HISK over the years, but also godmother, midwife, and general good conscience of the place. Isabel went above and beyond so many times that I can't do justice to the height and breadth of her commitment. To cite just one of many *largesses*: my talks were generally programmed in the evening, and Isabel not only made sure they ran smoothly and had an audience of residents, friends, and alumni, but would almost always attend, invariably order pizzas for afterward so that conversation could go on, and even help the last people standing to get home.

This project would not have been possible without the conversations, conviviality and expansive cooperation–but above all, the hard, creative, and convincing work–of the thirteen artists with and about whom I have written. In just a few weeks I reached out to and received generous and engaged feedback or suggestions from almost everyone. It was yet another reminder of why and how it is such a pleasure–as well as a challenge and a commitment–to talk through work.

Big and warm thanks, finally, to Freek Lomme at Set Margins' publications with whom I was chatting about an anthology of this kind earlier in the year. Freek's indefatigable energy and frank generosity saw it through . . . and brought it home.

We hope you enjoy these writings.

John C. Welchman, Los Angeles, August 2025

1. Friedrich Nietzsche, *Human All-Too-Human: A Book for Free Spirits*, Part II, trans. Paul V. Cohn (New York: The MacMillan Company, 1913), pp. 173-74; 182.

2. John C. Welchman, 'After the Wagnerian Bouillabaisse: Critical Theory and the Dada and Surrealist Word-Image,' in Judi Freeman, ed., *The Dada & Surrealist Word-Image* (exh. cat.) Los Angeles County Museum of Art, June 1989 (Cambridge, MA.: MIT Press), pp. 57-95; entries on 'Language,' 'Legacy,' Meaning,' 'Portraiture and Failed Portraiture,' 'Representation and Resemblance,' 'Self-Reference and Self-Portraiture,' 'Shop Window Display,' and 'Titles' for the exhibition catalogue *René Magritte: The Pleasure Principle*, Tate Liverpool, June to October 2011; Albertina, Vienna, November 2011 to February 2012, pp. 92-94, 95-96, 106-8, 141-47, 158-60, 164-65, 166-68, 170-75; '"An Original Arpocryphum" for Ricardo Brey' in *Qué Le Importa Al Tigre Una Raya Más: The Futility of Good Intentions*, curated by Bart de Baer, Museo Nacional de Bellas Artes de La Habana and Museum van Hedendaagse Kunst, Antwerp (Mer Paper Kunsthalle, 2014), pp. 43-84; '"Streets I Never Thought I Shou[l]d Revisit": Ricardo Brey and Photography,' in *Adrift* (Ghent: MER [Borgerhoff & Lamberigt], 2019), English and German eds.; *Guillaume Bijl* (Zurich: JRP|Ringer, 2017); *Koen van den Broek: Out of Place* (Ghent: Borgerhoff & Lamberigts, 2023); *Marcel Broodthaers: Pense-Bête* [inaugural volume of UpClose series] (Ghent: SMAK, 2023).

3. The 'Global Adorno' conference was programmed at the University of Amsterdam in association with Amsterdam School for Cultural Analysis (ASCA); Amsterdam Centre for Globalisation Studies (ACGS); Institute for the Humanities, Simon Fraser University, Vancouver; and Department of Philosophy (UvA).

4. John C. Welchman, 'Names, *Écriture* and Enigma: Adorno on Art as Writing,' *Zeitschrift für Ästhetik und allgemeine Kunstwissenschaft* (Hamburg: Meiner Verlag, 2017), vol. 62, no. 1, 2017.

5. Michel de Montaigne, 'Of the Art of Conference,' *The Essays of Montaigne* [Complete], trans. Charles Cotton, ed. William Carew Hazlitt (1877); available at www.gutenberg.net. Montaigne suggests that 'the use of [conversation is] more sweet than of any other action of life' and that as opposed to 'the study of books' which is but 'a languishing and feeble motion that heats not . . . conversation teaches and exercises at once.'

6. Georg Wilhelm Friedrich Hegel, 'Preface: On Scientific Cognition,' to *Phenomenology of Spirit* [Phenomenologie des Geistes], trans. Arnold Vincent Miller (Oxford: Oxford University Press, 1977), p. 3.

7. Hegel, 'Preface', pp. 28-29. The professional stakes of philosophical discourse have clearly and dramatically shifted. In his essay on conversation, Montaigne insisted that 'I had rather my son should learn in a tap-house to speak, than in the schools to prate.'

8. Richard Huelsenbeck, 'First German Dada Manifesto' ('Collective Dada Manifesto') delivered at the I. B. Neumann Gallery, Berlin (February 1918); originally published in *Der Zweemann*, Hanover, ca. 1919, reissued in 1920 as 'Collective Dada

Manifesto' signed by Huelsenbeck, Tristan Tzara, Franz Jung, George Grosz, Marcel Janco, Raoul Hausmann, Hugo Ball, Pierre Albert-Birot, Hans Arp, et al. In Rose-Carol Washton Long, ed., *German Expressionism: Documents from the End of the Wilhelmine Empire to the Rise of National Socialism* (Berkeley, Los Angeles, London: University of California Press, 1993), pp. 267-69.

9. Naum Gabo and Anton Pevsner, 'The Realistic Manifesto,' originally published as a poster in Moscow, August 5, 1920, to accompany an open-air exhibition on Tverskoie Boulevard; trans. Gabo in Herbert Read, *Gabo: Constructions, Sculpture, Paintings, Drawings, Engravings* (Cambridge, MA: Harvard University Press, 1957).

10. Joseph Beuys, 'Not Just a Few Are Called, but Everyone,' interview with Georg Jappe, trans. John Wheelwright, *Studio International*, vol. 184, no. 950, London (December 1972), pp. 226-28.

11. Art & Language, 'Letter to a Canadian Curator,' written in January 1982 to accompany a showing of paintings from the 'Lenin/Pollock' series in the exhibition *Mannerism: A Theory of Culture* at the Vancouver Art Gallery (March 27, to April 25,); originally addressed to Jo-Anne Birnie Danzker, curator of the exhibition; reprinted as 'Letter to a Canadian Curator,' in *Art-Language*, vol. 5, no. 1, Banbury (October 1982), pp. 32-35.

12. The abbreviated version of the conversation is available at: https://www.pipaprize.com/wp-content/uploads/2023/04/Sofia-Caesar-Warmup-Maintenance-and-Breakdown-Conversation-with-John-C.-Welchman-Ana-Elisa-Cohen.docx.pdf.

Essays, Conversations, and Notes
on HISK laureates, 2016–23

John C. Welchman

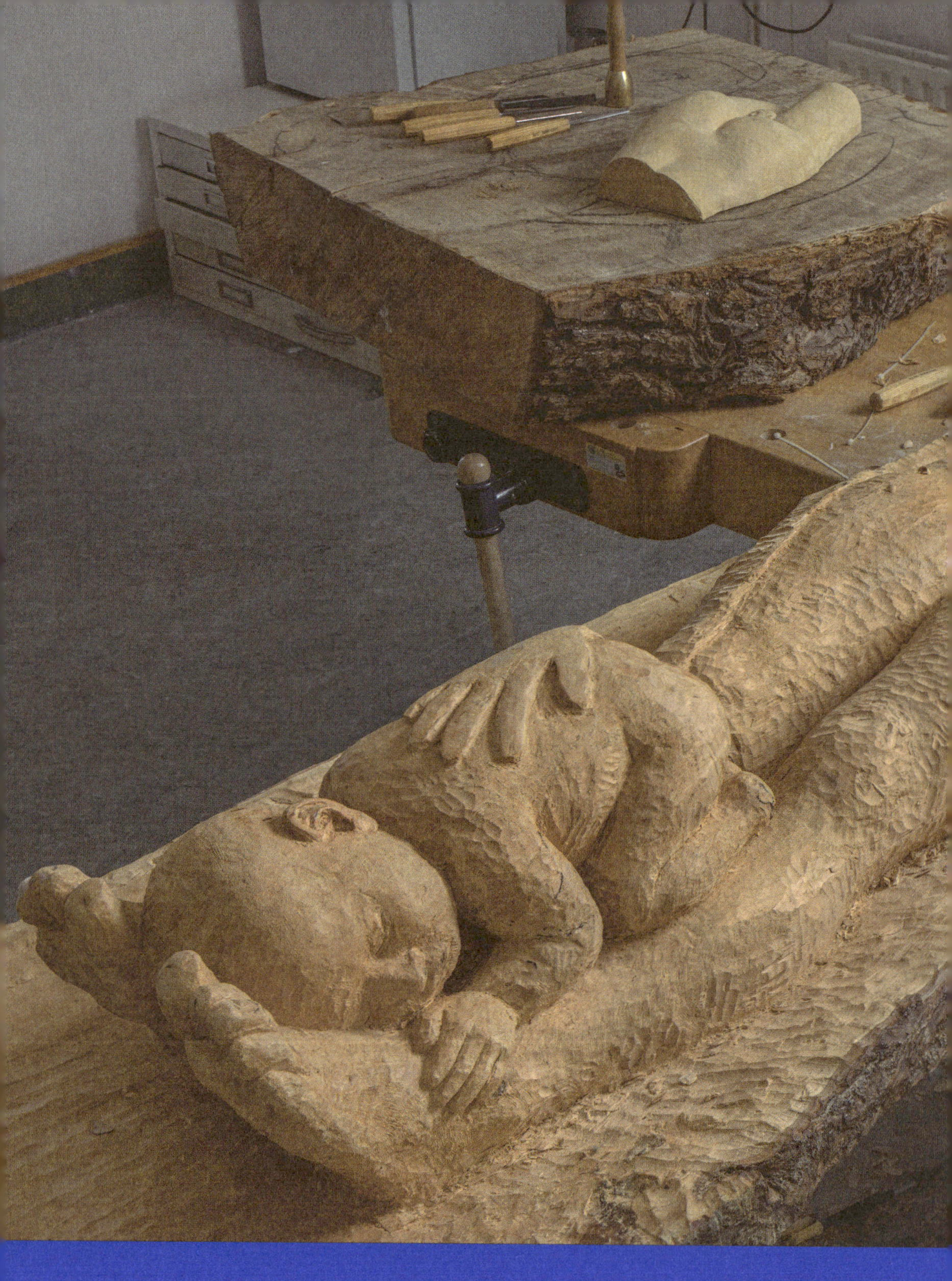

Femmy Otten, *Birthland*, 2025, limewood, 240 x 100 x 70 cm, courtesy the artist.
Photo: G.J. Van Rooij

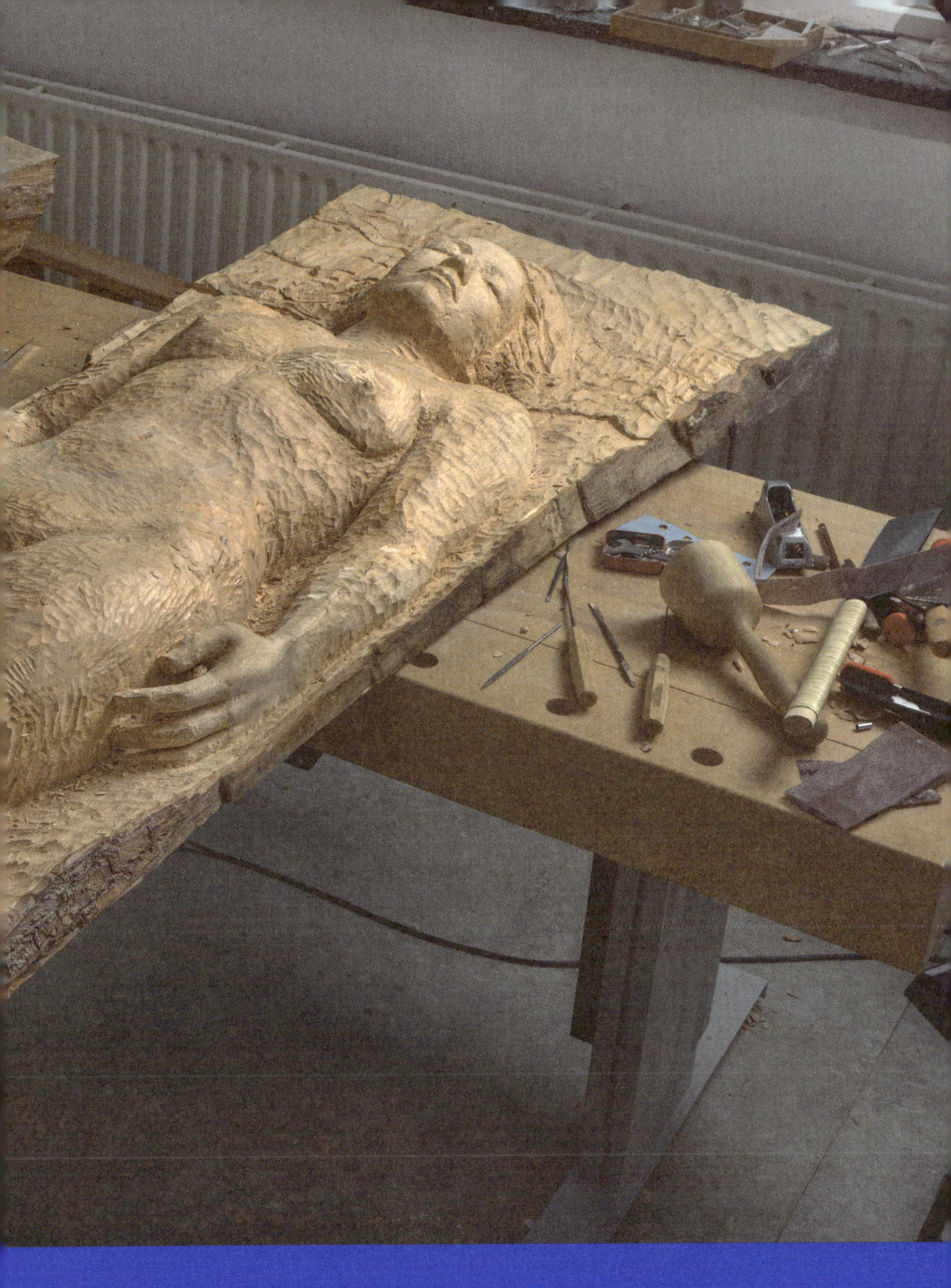

John C. Welchman (2025): Chronologically the first—as well as the most substantial—essay in this volume, 'What's a Head, or Afoot?: Femmy Otten's Partitive Aesthetics,' is based on conversations with Dutch artist Femmy Otten while she was at HISK (2009–10) and then Rijksakademie van beeldende kunsten, Amsterdam (2011–12), which were augmented by a long interview conducted in Amsterdam in May 2015 when I was commissioned to write an early-career overview for the monograph/catalogue/artist book Slow Down Love *(Rotterdam: Nai010, 2016) in association with an exhibition at Galerie Fons Welters, Amsterdam (September 10 to November 6, 2016). I shared illustrated lectures based on this essay at Rijksakademie (March 25, 2016) and at HISK—the latter part of a festive late-launch-cum-celebration of the book (September 5, 2017).*

On the Beginning

Raised by a police academy sports instructor and a nurse in a context where there was 'no art, at all . . . and also no music,' Femmy Otten sought refuge in the strange ease and immediacy of poetry, often reading Dutch poets, but also spending hours with Emily Dickinson. She feels as if she is 'standing close' to Dickinson's world—participating in the same sense of loneliness and longing, in the need to make free or to free up, in its exhilarating, sometimes excruciating, subtlety. But she is also infected by the palpable and recurrent disappointment ('a lot of disappointment') conjured up by Dickinson's writings and their inexorable meting-out of grief.[1] This turns, to be sure, on a version of the Romantic conundrum: that beauty is often sought by all—and craved by artists—but seldom, if ever, really, or fully, attained. The triangulation between desire, experience, and futility passes over into Otten's work not so much through her staging of aversion, but in what amounts to a representation of the loss of beautiful possibility. For Otten has come to realize that disappointment is animated by an intimate and disturbing form of self-consciousness in which the very pursuit of beauty is closed off. One of Otten's selves is nurtured in the ether of positive compromise—a self who already knows that she will not find what she at one point thought she wanted to seek out. While her sense of beauty has always been 'super-clear'; she is aware

What's a Head, or Afoot?:

Femmy Otten's Partitive Aesthetics

(to the point of abstinence) that when you 'reach' it, beauty might actually be 'so terribly boring.'[2]

Otten's work is framed, then, not by some kind of frustrated desire or corrupted idealism, but by fractures and cuts that manifest themselves in a defiantly partitive aesthetic predicated on psychological or cultural splits often articulated by hybrid and discontinuous forms. Its signature language is uttered through a crisis of eventuation manifest in the genres and materials of Otten's work, but also in its psychological and abstract dispositions. Things might start out, for example, as sculptures, but are–incompletely–carried on using lines or pigments. Figures often emerge from somewhere behind the wall or surface on which they are articulated and generally resolve only as corporeal part-objects–a disembodied head, arms, legs, body-on-body appurtenances. Or they are hybrids by nature, alluding to the rich history, consolidated in ancient Egyptian, Assyrian, and Greek cultures, of composite human-animal (centaur, sphinx, harpy, angel, and mermaid), non-human, animal-animal (griffin, chimera), or human-divine compounds–the latter including the theriocephalic ('beast-headed') gods and goddesses of the ancient Egyptians (such as Horus [falcon], Heqet [frog], and Bastet [cat]). For Otten, history itself is imagined as a series of thresholds and becomings that can be combined and subtracted in an idiosyncratic algebra of allusions so that they pronounce only on their lack of clarity and finality.

But Otten does not overindulge in the formal logic of the cut. Hers is not an art in which the processes of collage or montage are cheered on to some kind of self-referential finality. While certain things or appearances (lines, shapes, bodies) are, quite literally, cut or split, what results is not driven by technical protocols, but revealed, instead, by psychosocial experiences based on incommensurability and non-contiguity. Things don't fit together in the normal way because their fundamental syntax has been involuntarily scrambled. Which is not to say that Otten lacks awareness of the replicating non-finis that courses through her work. To the contrary, what she makes is charged up by the trail of potentials whose implications are evaporated as she shifts between forms, materials, and types, and, equally, between iconographies, ideas, and sensations. Otten never relinquishes full control over the future of her allusions, however. And it is for this reason that the *cadavre exquis* and its folded surprises offer a more plausible precedent than the cut-and-paste of the collage/montage model.

Otten works with observations and combinations developed not by making contact with something and then relinquishing it, but by starting out with various processes of detachment. This commitment extends to her relationship to portraiture, a genre she strives to separate from the assumptions ordered by identity, empathy, and completeness on which it has so often been predicated. Once again, it's not that Otten disregards–and then discards–the notion of em-pathy, for example, but that she has followed empathetic experience through to a certain point and then worked in the space where it might have continued, taken root, or somehow concluded. In its own way, but utterly without program or insistence, Otten's thoughts and motivations pass by some of the contemporary ideas caught up in the writings of the so-called 'Speculative Realists.' I am thinking, for example, of the call by Quentin Meillassoux in *After Finitude* to organize the search for an 'outside which thought could explore with the legitimate feeling of being on foreign territory–of being entirely elsewhere.'[3]

In what follows I take up with several of the points of con-tact that have initiated Otten's own beginnings. Operating, perhaps, in tandem with the pencils and crayons always left for the artist by her mother as she was growing up to 'calm her down'; they are moments or objects of concentration and precipitation. They launch vehicles and guidance devices that annotate a pursuit of beauty so uncoupled from 'sentiment' that it comes to resemble something else.

478–74 BCE: The *Charioteer* of Delphi (*Heniokhos [Ηνίοχος]*, the rein-holder)

Shortly after her parents divorced, when Otten was thirteen, her mother took Femmy and her two sisters to Greece as a kind of re-spite and compensation. Standing in the Delphi Archaeological Museum in front of the famous sculpture of a *Charioteer* on her latter-day Grand Tour, Otten could do nothing other than cry. Catching sight of her circumstances, a museum guard came up to her, she said, took her hand and ushered her forward with the whispered instruction that she should step over the safety cordon surrounding the sculpture and 'touch his feet'; Built on a sudden, overwhelming flush of emotion that ruined her adjudication of cause and effect, Otten's coming-of-

age story was propelled by a double scene of voyeurism
(as she was consumed with looking while being watched)
layered over an involuntary surrender to transgressive
instruction, and orchestrated by the multiple consquen-
ces of *being touched*-as emotion welled up, inexplicably;
as she is physically touched . . . and led; and as she
becomes the perpetrator of another touch-of the charioteer's foot-that closes the experience by opening up another world. After Otten withdrew from her illicit prox-
imity to the slender, bare feet, hemmed off just above
the ankle by the columnar folds of the figure's tunic,
she looked at her mother, 'a very practical lady,' with
an expression that asked for 'more time.' This she was
granted and 'that'; she says, 'was the start everything'
. . . and it 'was beautiful.'

But not beautiful in the swoop, swoon, and surrender
sense. And not beautiful because of the enlightenment
conferred by an uplifting encounter with Classical
Greek art. For here Otten thinks with a slightly more
expansive variant of the ineluctably 'base' concentration of André Boiffard and Georges Bataille in 1929:
to the big toes they isolate as fetishized taboos,[4] she
retorts, 'It was the foot.' She attached herself, then,
to part of a body that is both incomplete in itself
(the charioteer is missing his left forearm, silver
eyelashes, and other details on the head-though, almost
uniquely, he retains his inlaid glass eyes) and consti-
tutes, in turn, a fragment of the original sculptural
whole. The 'original' included the competition chariot
that won a race at the Pythian Games, held at Delphi
every four years in honor of Pythian Apollo,and its
team of either four or six horses, parts of which were
found on site. From another point of view, Otten took
up with the feet of a figure not much older than she
was at the time, probably a noble, teenaged jockey in
charge of a top-of-the-line team of chariot and horses
supplied by and representing a rich Sicilian city. Then

again, she touched what was in reach of her touch, the very pivot of balance and control that coordinates the implicit kinetic energy of the larger sculptural whole–signaled by the handling of the reins and the focus of the eyes. For Otten, the feet were the point, but also the potential, of the work.

Reflecting on the episode later, Otten immediately invoked the shadow it cast over her everyday life in the years that followed, recalling that the shape of a coffee machine in the house in which she was raised was articulated with similar oval shapes–as were the cookies she ate at her grandma's house: 'The graduation of the forms,' she notes, 'was just the same.' For Otten, these conjunctions and replays and the rapprochements they stage between history and experience are the real sites of her 'happiness' as an artist. They represent the only kind of coming together she can really imagine. They are the only way she can keep abreast of what's afoot.

First Half of the Twelfth Century and Later: Figures and Heads at Angkor Wat

A decade or so ago, Otten went to Cambodia to visit the temple complex at Angkor Wat. She was transfixed not by the astonishing scale of the site or the teeming multiplicity of its sculptures, but by one form of generalized affect that overwhelmed her experience. It arrived as soon as she 'saw their smiles, the most mysterious smiles you can ever imagine.'

An imaginary history of the smile offers a counterpoint to the transhistorical constellation of Otten's own revelations, crossing over with these at several moments. The so-called 'archaic smile,' quite widespread in Greek sculpture, especially in *kouroi* (statues of young men) made during the second quarter of the sixth century BCE–around a hundred years before the *Charioteer*, though the smile persevered into the beginning of the Classical era–was probably used as an indicator of vivacity or well-being, summed up in the Greek notion of *agalma*, 'the life affirming capacity to delight by means of sheer beauty.'[5] Interpretations of the archaic smile are wildly divergent, ranging from the pressures of anatomical accident or the naïve striving for 'naturalism' to the cosmologically tinged metaphysics advanced by John Fowles in his novel *The Magus*.[6] Fowles extrapolates from the meager predicate of these upwardly curled archaic lips to pronounce them redolent of 'the purest metaphysical good humour . . . timelessly intelligent and timelessly amused. . . .

Because a star explodes and a thousand worlds like ours die, we know this world is. That is the smile: that what might not be, is.'[7] His rhetoric notwithstanding, Fowles catches here something essential not only to Otten's attraction to representations of the smile, but to her aesthetic as a whole. Only the terms are reversed, for Otten is more likely to parse the smile as an indicator of fracture, not reparation, standing for something that 'is, but might not be.'

The enigmatic reflexivity of the sculptural smiles at Angkor Wat may relate, with reasonable directness, to the diffusion of Greek influence into Central Asia beginning in the fourth century BCE. But the more immediate Hindu, and later Buddhist, religious and iconographic contexts of the figures in the temple complex clearly reorient the implications of these visages. This is attested most vividly in the teeming multiplicity of *apsaras* (female spirits of the clouds and waters) and *devata* (lesser deities) that adorn the temple galleries. The former, associated with an elegance and sensuality often manifest in dance, exemplified for Otten a particularly redolent concentration of seductive, motile form that was also transient and otherworldly. The smiles of these beings seemed to layer immediate pleasure with intimations of a larger purpose while never giving away their secrets. They are emblematic of a pantheist abundance and decorous corporeal abandon largely absent in the tradition of Christian sculpture from the Middle Ages to the early Renaissance that was also of great importance to the artist. The smiling *apsaras* offered, then, a communion between reflex and desire, on the one hand, and inner comportment or preternatural confidence on the other—a portal to the deeper conjunction of mind and body that has always been a source of wonder, and doubt, for Otten.

Each of Otten's points of departure—whether in classical Greek sculpture, the Hindu and Buddhist pantheons of Angkor Wat, Indian sculptures, or portraiture before Raphael—is deeply implicated in religious and mystical concerns. Yet Otten is far from 'enthusiastic' about the monopoly often sought by organized religion over the terms—and experience—of mythology or ritual. For her, rituals are invented 'to deal with taboos' but then become entrenched in dogma. Raised in the orbit of Dutch Protestantism, Otten's 'love' for rituals brought her into contact with the Catholic church and later with other religions, which she encountered not in their privileged books or written doctrines, but through the refracting prism of the sculptural forms to which they gave rise. Otten's work does not, therefore, advocate for or espouse religious views so much as it visualizes certain forms and moments of 'dedication.'

1435–1440: Rogier van der Weyden, *Portrait of a Young Women* [or *Lady Wearing a Gauze Headdress*]

Otten's encounter with van der Weyden's portrait of a young woman wearing a plain, white hennin, or headdress (now in the Gemäldegalerie, Berlin), was another of those 'magical' experiences that have punctuated her career. In this case, the artist was mesmerized by certain technical effects used by Van der Weyden to manage the presence and appearance of light. Chief among these is the force of the picture's illumination, which, Otten noted, seems to 'come from inside the painting.' While the actual source of light in the picture is delivered–with the insistence of a studio spotlight–from almost directly overhead, the fierce whites of the starched linen folds and the whitish pink of the woman's features appear to be self-irradiated as the flanking wings of the headdress and the ruffles of the scarf around her neck act like a reflection box, harvesting and re-diffusing the play of light over the subject's fabric-framed features. These effects are multiplied and transposed by further rounds of technical finesse as 'the light reflects on the white under-painting through the different transparent layers.'

As with all her icons; other aspects of the oak panel painting relate to the choices and dilemmas in Otten's work. The palpable vivacity of the sitter's eyes–typical of Van der Weyden's earlier portraits–is underscored by their intense *contrapposto* gaze, which makes a kind of psychological right angle with the left-facing inclination of her head, creating a matrix of alertness and presence. But this inner liveliness is absorbed by the calculated sobriety of the woman's fur-lined, pewter-collared gown with its ample sleeves and pleated bodice, the social rectitude of her piously clasped hands and the radiant modesty of her spotless hennin. These oppositions, fundamental to Otten's sense of women in her representations of the world, play out in a different way in the uncertainty surrounding the sitter's identity. Some scholars have posited that the portrait represents the artist's wife, Elisabeth Goffaert,[8] while others suggest Nicole du Bosquiel, one of the mistresses of Philip III (known as 'The Good'), duke of Burgundy (1396–1467).[9]

The equivocations occasioned by *Portrait of a Young Women* between notions of expressive and submissive selfhood, or, more literally, between the good wife and a courtly mistress, gave rise to what Otten notes was her own sense of relativity when viewing 'the painting many times': on each occasion 'it told me something else.' However, the possibilities unfurled during these encounters were not simply a product of the formal and iconographical complexities of the work itself, but arose, she reports, 'because I was changed . . . every time the painting brought me another shock.' The engorged luminosity of the panel coupled with its possession by two putatively opposite female types, mother and concubine, granted a kind of permission, then, for Otten to stage various readings charged by the interleaving of the painting's own power and her shifting circumstances. The resulting spectrum of associations funded by the intensities of her aesthetic encounters is a model of her general adjudication between personal experience and artistic languages, between imagination and history, indulgence and restraint, light and dark, self and other.

After 1457: Piero della Francesca, *Madonna del Parto*

The woman depicted in relief emerging from the wall in Otten's *New Myth for New Family* (2011) quotes, quite directly, Piero della Francesca's *Madonna del Parto*, finished, according to Vasari, when the artist visited his dying mother in Sansepolcro in 1459. In Piero's painting the Madonna's hand is posed over her pregnant stomach, but in Otten's her entire body below the chest is missing; while the hands and fingers, lacking the corporeal supports of the original, now appear discomfortingly twisted. This is a radical gesture–the more so in light of the painting's title, which associates the work with the development of a new mythology organized on behalf of a renovated conception of the family. What are we to make of the artist's removal of the organs of generation on behalf of her alternative genealogy? Is it an attempt to circumvent the defining symbolic maternality of the Madonna, to outbid the virginity of Mary by absconding with her womb? Is it a liberating gesture that subtracts the possessive directives of biology from the production of human subgroups? Or a bid for cosmic or cyborg engendering? As ever in Otten's work, the answer is neither obvious or certain, nor is it necessarily couched in such grandiose terms.

We find a clue in the other elements of *New Myth for New Family* and the syntax that organizes their parts. To the (viewer's) right of the Pieroesque woman are two other portraits probably based on Otten's sister.[10] The appearance of these figures aligns them less with the ethos of the mid-fifteenth century than with later imaginations of how portraits might have been managed in the era before Raphael. While they have lesser volumes of flowing hair and their lips are not quite so plump, the women resemble the female portraits painted by members of the Pre-Raphaelite Brotherhood, founded in 1848 by William Holman Hunt, John Everett Millais, and Dante Gabriel Rossetti. They share the same half-closed, hooded eyes and blank expressions as well as the preference for three-quarter profiles and certain similarities in subject matter—a focus on purity, spirituality, and love.[11]

That the pair is indicated as some form of progeny or kin of the sculpted women—whether artistic or biological—is confirmed by the trajectory of the multi-colored connection line that both stabilizes and segments the wall-bound parts of this work. Like genealogical brackets, this device runs from below the larger portrait and to the left of its companion to connect with a vertical line that descends from the base of the relief figure, passing, on the way, a Philip Guston–like patch of abstract paint marks and a more defined sequence of some eight color swatches marked onto the wall directly under the right hand of the figure, like a rank of supplemental fingers. To the left of the relief figure, where the line turns aquamarine, three drawn arrows (of the weaponry not indicating kind) point upward, while a small painting of disappearing linear marks is tucked under the line in the corner formed by its right-angled turn. From this point the line travels horizontally, terminating at an arrowhead that forms the tip of a reddish-pink, snake-cum-penis—resembling those standing in for genitals in the sculptural figures of *Yellow Minutes* (2012). Two final elements are drawn and sculpted onto the wall above the line at the left extremity of the work: first, a galloping horse transformed into a centaur through the addition of a puppet-like, red-domed head apparently wearing a crown, on which a gun-toting figure rides; and, secondly, another, smaller, female bas-relief sporting wings with multi-colored feathers.

The complex disposition of *New Myth for New Family* is clearly posed in dialogue with the spatial and iconographical organization of the *Madonna del Parto*. The right-angled line that traverses Otten's work is her version of the diameter-like cross section that cuts through Piero's tent and doubles up on the theatrical openings that mark the earlier painting—of the tent itself, dramatically cinched and 'revealed' by the two angels—and the startling, slightly zigzag, rift that runs through the mid-section of the Madonna's gorgeously ample *blu oltremare* gown. The symmetry of the flanking angels—specular reflections executed using the same perforated cartoons—carries over into Otten's work in the fugal arrangement of its own pairs: the two female portraits to the right; the couple constituted by the female relief and her painted cameo; and the further duos on the left side of the work—the human heads of the 'horse' and its rider and the angel and centaur themselves. Further, Piero's three protagonists are echoed by Otten's three arrows; while its hidden fourth, represented by the unborn Christ, is wittily parodied by the penis-form snake that launches the directional vectors of *New Myth for New Family* with comically insistent, disembodied masculine bravado.

Otten repossesses and augments the apparatuses and allegorical finesse of the *Madonna del Parto*, extemporizes on the pathos of its place in Piero's life (completed in the village of his birth as his mother died), and interleaves all this in a leperello of historical, aesthetic, and religious references from which formalized theologies are expelled. She uses polychromatic punctuation, for example, to secure a certain measure of lucidity in the work's syntax of parts. The dashes of a multihued halo set above the main sculptural figure join with the differential spectrum of the genealogical line, the chromatic pluralism of the feathered wings, the patchwork coloring of the centaur, with the tints of the arrows, and finally with the more abstract color swatches and 'exercises' set under the main figure, almost in lieu of her missing body. These moments of chromatic intensity–perhaps most abundant in *New Myth for New Family*–are recurrent in Otten's work. Three of the wall-bound sculptural figures of *The Seven Joys of Mary* (2010), for example, are bracketed by a pair of color devices: the first, a vagrant color circle inset with triangular wedges of different colors; the second, a parenthesis of three monochrome shapes–an irregular, six-sided form, a thin, blue sliver that acts as the fulcrum or 'bend' for the group, and a slightly non-conforming red rectangle.

Another congregation of triangles, this time red and pink, are painted at the lowest extremity of Otten's plaster, oil color, and tempera wall installation *Untitled* (2012). In *The Eternal Hunting Field* (2014) these italicizations of color are offset by emphases elsewhere in Otten's work on grisaille or monochromatic appearance, spare penciled outlines, white plaster modeling, or the effects of natural wood grains–as in *If You Were Coming in the Fall* (2012) and her 2014 exhibition *And Life Is Over There*, for example. Other paintings and hybrid sculpture-drawings work with a reduced color range, limited to pale greens and blues.

In *New Myth for New Family*, Otten also detours Piero's iconography, crossing Greek mythological fauna with Catholic Mariology, layering intimations of pagan fertility rites with the Immaculate Conception, rhyming Roman with Renaissance. Details set into the background of the two painted portraits bring Otten's revisions of color and content together. Over the head of one portrait Otten adds three small, heraldic constellations of yellow and pink dots and colored circles somehow linked together with runic concentration. This figure also clutches a fish in each of the hands attached to a pair of wildly disproportionate spider-like arms that sprout from its neck, a more orthodox Christian symbol for Christ the signification of which is reinforced by the inscription

of a Greek 'R' nearby, part of the ancient Chi Rho
Christogram. The second portrait is surmounted by five
green dots with blank centers that act like thought bubbles or an extended ellipsis; while her neck is adorned
with green dotted lines that form a schematic necklace,
and her left shoulder marked with a brooch-like decora-
tion consisting of a red spiral on a white ground
flanked by six pink and green 'solar rays.'

Circa 1450–1550: German Limewood Sculpture

When she carves her wooden heads, faces, and figures
Otten emphasizes their provisionality, giving them different levels of finish, imbuing them with the condition
of their apparent emergence from the wall, as if their
non finis surfaces were created in the effort of dragging
them forth. To do otherwise, Otten ventures, would confer
upon them the transient vulnerability of being 'too beautiful.' Deferring is thus essential, for as Dickenson
wrote in the poem that titled Otten's exhibition at Fons
Welters in 2014: 'Life is over there –   / Behind the
Shelf.'[12] These hesitations are fueled by a kind of self-
directed anger arising from Otten's awareness that even
while using the same materials as the great limewood
masters of the later fifteenth and early sixteenth centuries she could never achieve—at least not in the same
terms-the kind of 'direct formal language' they mustered.

One is tempted to read the menacing array of oversized
knives and forks posed with a dose of Magrittean mischief
in front of a house and its beautifully articulated,
tree-lined garden in an untitled painting from 2014 as
a commentary on the allures and impossibilities of carving, incising, and cutting up. It is not surprising,
then, that strategies of 'detouring' join with those
informing the cut or the part in order that the artist
can face in the right direction for the telling of her
'stories.'

This might also account for the fact that while Otten
admires the sculptures of Tilman Riemenschneider (ca.

1460–1531) and deems his 'skills so amazing,' she does not quite love his figures and finds it difficult to empathize with them. Perhaps, like Michael Baxandall, she detects 'something of a trick, if a great one' in the 'unremitting but indeterminate' pathos of Riemenschneider's art.[13]   Better, from her point of view, is the work of late Gothic Swabian master Gregor Erhart, especially his limewood *Saint Mary Magdalene* (ca. 1515–20, Louvre), a work 'so sensitive, so clear and so soft' that 'the way she looks at us' offers up silence on behalf of presence. If it was the feet of the *Charioteer* of Delphi that gripped her as an adolescent, now Mary Magdalene's knees—one weight-bearing and flexed, the other slightly bent, both fringed by the outrageous tresses of the repentant ascetic–bring forth only exclamation: 'tja. . . wow.' As her eyes are downcast, signifying transport, her breasts partly obscured and her feet slightly flat and remote, it is the saint's knees that stand in for all of these corporeal pairs and sum them up.

Remonstrating with her self-directed anger, Otten's version of the anxiety of influence, the artist conjures up another veiled motivation that cuts across and interferes with those I have already outlined. This arrives in the immediacy of ultra-direct expression, the capacity to make and mean without any 'trappings or frills.' In Otten's view, certain moments in Western art history come closest to this unflinching directness, including the visual language of much Roman art and the work of various, so-called 'outsiders' such as that of the self-taught Alabaman Bill Trayor (1854–1949).[14] For her part, Otten acknowledges not only that she needs 'a big detour to reach a direct image' but also that she is highly attuned to the perception of both the direct and more mediated aspects of this quality in other artists. 'I saw the Fra' Angelicos in [the Convent and Museum of] San Marco in Florence,' she notes, 'and in him I recognized the same fascination that Henry Darger [1892–1973] has for me. They also need hours of perusal and reflection in order to reach this direct image, and both have this almost autistic precision built into their world as it is manifest in their works.'

Not surprisingly, Otten is also committed to something that amounts to the opposite of this long-form journey into meaning: a mode of expression that activates or anticipates the references to performative actions–riding, dancing, even flow diagrams–that accumulate in her work between sculpture and painting. Perhaps this is a means of compensating for the static appearance of her portraits and the stop-action declensions of her chosen media. But if some of these devices–such as the inclusion in a few installations or studio photographs of a phantom visiting figure tumbling or doing a headstand–seem like over-deliberated supplements, in other instances they have thickened into a performative substrate that takes command of the twisting axes of limewood sculpture and then stands (or moves) on its own. This is nowhere more apparent than with the performance *The Restless Gods*, produced during the opening of Otten's exhibition at Fons Welters in 2014, the 'need' for which she 'felt so clearly.'

'With the performance I wanted to connect with something wild, ancient,' Otten stated, 'I wanted to sidestep the dichotomy between rationality and mysticism, in a way.' The performance evokes, reproduces, and simulates the vertigo induced by spinning, and thus joins with a genealogy of inquiries into vertiginous effects that includes, perhaps most notably, Paul McCarthy's *Spinning* (1970).[15] Otten's performance is strictly graduated so that the dancer's turns are kept under control, slowly accelerating until the frenetic spins of the last thirty seconds or so. At this point, the dancer becomes almost unraveled or unbound, and it seems that her figure is destined to fly off like a model helicopter or bore into the ground like a renegade mine bit. Recognizably, but not ostentatiously 'feminine,' the Lithuanian-born performer Lora Juodkaite wears not an overdramatized, flowing dress or billowing scarves in the Isadora Duncan tradition, but rather understated clothing that trains the viewer's attention on the deformation of her body. She takes instruction to move 'within herself' by performing turns for about ten minutes . . . in what ensues as a subtly incremental crescendo. The music used as a counterpoint to the dance was originally a recording by Benjamin Britten, but Otten changed the setup to feature a live instrumentalist, Peter Le Feber, who improvised on the oboe. Le Feber ends on a high note and then relinquishes the sonic dimension of the piece to the light steps and deep breaths of the dancer. Otten is especially concerned here with what she terms 'de-dramatization'–not conducted with a tendentious, Brecht-like rigor, but coiled up in the unfussily practical mise-en-scène and everyday attire, which couples with studied introspection in such a way that the performance reaches the threshold of a release that never comes–though the quality of that release is nevertheless palpable. 'You need the beginning for all this at the end,' Otten suggests, 'you need to make a place in people's heads.'

The performance responds to the artist's desire to precipitate interplay between images and objects, sound and performance. To this end, the twist or crook of the dancer's arms is reprised in the exhibited sculptures. Because Otten understands the body as 'a source of knowledge'–rather than as spectacle, reflection, and desire–she felt that her work 'had become more alive by these means.' She invests in the invention of rituals, which are always there even if they are not explicitly represented.

So, in addition to contemporary art world precedents, such as McCarthy's, *The Restless Gods* looks to real-world models, including the whirling in remembrance of God (or *dhikr*) of the Sama ceremony performed by the Sufi Mevlevi Order founded in Konya (then capital of the Anatolian Seljuk Sultanate) by followers of Jalal ad-Din Muhammad Balkhi-Rumi, the thirteenth-century Persian poet, Islamic jurist, and theologian. In addition to these more literal and metaphysical twists, however, something still remains of the sinuousness of the late Gothic tradition and even of the various roundnesses that inhabit the *Madonna del Parto*: the circular pavilion or tent on the diameter of which the Virgin and her flanking angels are arranged, as well as the roundness of pregnancy and 'expectation' themselves.

1986: Andrei Tarkovsky, *Sculpting in Time*

The plastic intensity of German limewood sculpture also gives onto and illuminates another defining commitment of Otten's work: her opening-up of the relationship between sculpture and painting, and the conjunction of both with temporality, an exploration that more than any other informs her signature style. The elastic but exacting give and take between these genres–along with questions about relationality in general–are present in almost all her gallery-installed work, but especially clear, perhaps, in *Yellow Minutes*. Here, the figures are locked into their dispositions and becomings by processes of commission that don't quite 'take.' They seem to gesture toward a leap, a dance, or a fall without viewers believing or imagining that they are actually doing these things. They appear to be somewhat 'left in the lurch,' on the one hand, while possessed of mischievous demeanors reminiscent of satyrs or bacchants, on the other, complete with snake-like genitalia and a generically 'Mediterranean' appearance. Catching things and people at the threshold of action, but stopping them short of what might be expected of or predicted from a gesture or historical stereotype, is, in part at least, a consequence of Otten's equivocation between something fully formed (say, sculpture in the round) and something flat or abstracted. But the effect is accentuated by the artist's delivery to her multipart wall and floor pieces of a suggestive syntax of correlations, analogues, and logical aporia built from doubling, duplication, and repetition–of heads, arms, colors, emblems, origins, and textures.

Commenting on the work that led up to *Yellow Minutes*, Otten points, again, to a certain failure prompted by her loss of time: 'I had an urge for something and I didn't find it.' Her response was to clear everything away and try again 'at the last moment.' Trial and error followed by cancellation or erasure is key to the way Otten is able to go forward. 'I always find myself building up to that specific moment in which something is going happen,' she notes, 'I always feel–with Emily Dickinson–that's it's a question of a state of mind rather than a state of thinking–a [mental ambience] that's so hard to find, so rare, I feel. But then sometimes it rushes in . . . it can be there in a minute after half a year of waiting. I am addicted to this waiting-out,' she adds, 'and the pay-off is that you know with utter security when the right thing has emerged. Though there's no trick involved in getting there.' Her aim is to win the battle with the kind of 'trickery' or emotional deception that Baxandall found in Riemenschneider's sculptures: to wait out, rather than almost to extort, the possibilities of making.

The long and shorter-form temporalities that Otten considers here are crucial. Her working process involves extended periods of mental and physical preparation in the studio 'and then I take it to the exhibition space and sit with it as long as necessary.' Here, she waits, 'sometimes in an almost trance-like state, for the energy of the associations I have made to return to the work and enter the space. The process is complete when there is no need for patience anymore, it's just energy. From this 'functional' moment I can work on details, paint or draw things on the walls.' Otten's sculpting of–and with–time has implications for other aspects of her work, beginning with a central claim: that what she makes 'is not a depiction of my world, it is my world.' In this sense, Otten steps out of time–making, waiting, delaying, and then seizing–only to return to the temporal footprint of the immediately 'real.' She therefore describes herself as a 'magical thinker'–in part 'because there was no place for this in my family'; but also because of the time-driven accumulations that inhabit her figures, mysterious hybrids–self-portraits, family members, political personae, mytho-logical human-animal compounds, all loosely recognizable and most supplied with common features–almond eyes, arched brows, smooth mouse-like skin. In these figures what is closest to the artist is admixed with elements that are historically or religiously remote. She invariably starts 'with a specific model, most often my sister (though a bit less frequently now).' Or with herself for her last sculpture, *And Life Is Over There* (2014) and for 'several male fi-gures in my paintings.' In order to reach for a point of commence-ment in this initial phase, she asserts: 'I just need somebody.' Of course, what was most immediate to Otten was the figure with

whom she has spent the most time in her life, her younger
sister: 'My sense of fascination started with her, I was always looking at her face and I couldn't stop thinking about
it, how the graduations between its parts were possible.'
The familiarity, but also unending formal complexity, of her
sister's visage 'can still calm me down,' she notes, 'if I'm
lying in bed, upset, I feel the form of her face, but also
of my sculpture/portrait, in my body.' It is in her sister,
and her uncanny twin (herself), that the long and short contingencies of time are overlaid and united.

A second implication of Otten's work with time arises from
another mode of hybridization that informs and builds on
that of her figures: a largely intergeneric practice articulated between painting and sculpture. Otten is the first to
acknowledge the difference between these genres, but does so
by emphasizing, yet again, their temporal disarticulation.
While painting involves a completely different kind of energy, she is drawn, time and again, to the remorseless accumulation of 'associations' that arise from her sculptural process. So much so that 'the sculptures,' she admits, just have
to be made and therefore 'sometimes ruin my life . . . I
work on something for five months and change it, it's a different level of adventure.' For Otten, paintings are 'more
additive' as they attempt to 'complete the world.' But even
if paintings can be 'too talkative,' and sculptures 'too ob-
trusive,' their interaction is both necessary and inevitable
to her way of representing.

The third implication to which I want to point here concerns the quietly willful gender-indeterminacy associated
with many of her figures that couple with larger instabili-
ties of the subjects in and of representation. More a product of how the artist observes and understands human nature
than a deliberate attempt to create role reversals, Otten
proposes the re-dressing of a world that is already crossed.
She attributes the cause of this reorientation to a form of
reparation, something that might be made good by time, but
only when stretched out to infinity: 'Maybe this is another
aspect of my continual search for completeness in my work;
though it's also a token of my disappointment as I always
believe what I do is going to be complete and then somehow

it isn't.' Personal relations cut across this consideration, as they did in the question of genre. For Otten makes an important distinction between her disavowal of 'the personal' and her pedagogic commitment to helping young artists pursue their self-directed searches: 'I always tell my students to keep as close to their selves as possible.' Otten is aware that it's too easy just to claim that 'the closer you come to yourself, the more universal it becomes.' for she is unwilling to foreclose her desire 'to create out of my innermost self, without confusion.' Time is the chief agent that secures the difference between these categories, for: 'The inner self is not the same as the personal: the personal doesn't interest me because it is not resistant in itself–it is always an explanation, or sometimes an excuse.' We arrive here at one of the questions with which Otten's work is most preoccupied: 'How [to] give form to what goes beyond the here and the now . . . how can I make a transhistorical work in my time, with my time.'

One solution was suggested as Otten read Andrei Tarkovsky's posthumously published reflections on the temporalities of film and art, *Sculpting in Time*.[16] Even the title of this volume intervenes in the questions before us here, as the Russian *Запечатлённое время* might be translated, more literally, as 'Depicted Time'–offering another 'take' on the relations between time and dimensionality, representation and depiction. Tarkovsky's meditations gathered around the renovation of an older concept that allowed him to think through the relations between personal and historical ideas, symbols, and forms–and the scenes of their communication and recognition. He was concerned, like Otten, with how the work of art could confer on its audience some kind of liberating experience or release– how, as Otten puts it, what is made is also a revelatory 'addition to what might have come, what might be coming.' Tarkovsky's version of 'catharsis' turns on forms of shock that are powerful and unremitting. The cathartic is an experience that reveals in an art work its own consciousness and spiritual power, a place where two desires–the artist's and the viewer's–converge to set, and make, something free: it is a moment of mutual discovery and of recognition for the feeling of expanded feelings. 'Like Dostoevsky,' Otten suggests, 'he builds his films towards catharsis, making space in the reader's head . . . just as I tried to do in my performance by building up to the 'silent' moment where you only hear breath and feet.' Here is the adventure of Otten's work, the culmination of so much time ('hours spent carving or painting, awaiting a moment of clarity that is so exciting'): it is, finally, a way to make things that 'cannot lie.'

1. See, 'I Measure Every Grief I meet' (poem 561), in *The Complete Poems of Emily Dickinson*, ed. Thomas H. Johnson (New York: Little, Brown, 1976), pp. 428-29.

2. Unless otherwise indicated, Otten is quoted from an interview with the author conducted at the Rijksakademie van Beeldende Kunsten, Amsterdam, May 12, 2015; or from email correspondence with the author exchanged between May and September 2015.

3. Quentin Meillassoux, *After Finitude: An Essay on the Necessity of Contingency* (London: Bloomsbury, 2009), p. 7.

4. Three full page photographs of big toes by Jacques-André Boiffard (*Gros orteil, sujet masculine, 30 ans; Gros orteil, sujet masculine, 29 ans;* and *Gros orteil, sujet féminin, 24 ans,* all 1929), were published in *Documents*, vol. 1, no. 6, November 1929, pp. 298-99, along with a text by Georges Bataille titled 'Le Gros Orteil.' See, Raymond Spiteri, 'Georges Bataille and the Limits of Modernism,' *emaj*, no. 4 (2009), pp. 1-27, https://emajartjournal.files.wordpress.com/2012/08/spiteri.pdf.

5. See, Angus Trumble, *A Brief History of the Smile* (New York: Basic Books, 2004), esp. pp. 10-18; here p. 14.

6. For another account of the impact of smiling and mirth, see Leah S. Marcus, *The Politics of Mirth: Jonson, Herrick, Milton, Marvell, and the Defense of Old Holiday Pastimes* (Chicago: University of Chicago Press, 1989).

7. John Fowles, *The Magus* (London: Pan Books, 1968 [1965]), p. 133.

8. For a discussion of this attribution, see Christa Grössinger, *Picturing Women in Late Medieval and Renaissance Art* (Manchester: Manchester University Press, 1997), p. 60.

9. See, Albert Châtelet, *Rogier van der Weyden: problèmes de la vie et de l'oeuvre* (Strasbourg: Presses Universitaires de Strasbourg, 1999), pp. 112-114.

10. A snapshot of Otten's studio, posted on the artist's website, makes this association clear.

11. Examples might include: William Holman Hunt, *Portrait of Fanny Holman Hunt* (1866-1867); and Dante Gabriel Rossetti, *Regina Cordium* (1866) and *Lady Lilith* (1866-68, 1872-73).

12. Otten's exhibition *And Life Is Over There* was at the Fons Welters gallery, Amsterdam in 2014; Dickinson's poem 'I Cannot Live with You' (poem 604) is collected in *The Complete Poems of Emily Dickinson*, ed. Thomas H. Johnson (New York: Little, Brown, 1976), pp. 492-93.

13. Noted by Henri Zerner, 'Masterwoodworks,' *New York Review of Books*, December 18, 1980, review of Michael Baxandall, *The Limewood Sculptors of Renaissance Germany* (New Haven: Yale University Press, 1982).

14. See, Josef Helfenstein and Roman Kurzmeyer, eds., *Deep Blues: Bill Traylor, 1854-949* (New Haven: Yale University Press, 1999).

15. I note elsewhere that in his early work Paul McCarthy destabilized the 'architectural specificity' of the studio as 'both viewer and artist/performer [were] subject to several forms of disequilibrium, including the vertigo that attended the 30 to 40 minute duration of *Spinning* (1970) in which the studio is made over as a centrifuge for the production of disorientation, giving rise to a series of perceptual inquiries that culminates in the eerie, silent list of *The Box* (1999).' See, John C. Welchman, *Catching Mayhem by Its Tale*, vol. 2 of *Paul McCarthy: Caribbean Pirates* (Zurich: Hauser & Wirth, 2020).

16. Andrei Tarkovsky, *Sculpting in Time: Reflections on the Cinema*, trans. Kitty Hunter-Blair (Austin: University of Texas Press, 1987). The book was first published in German in 1986, shortly after Tarkovsky's death.

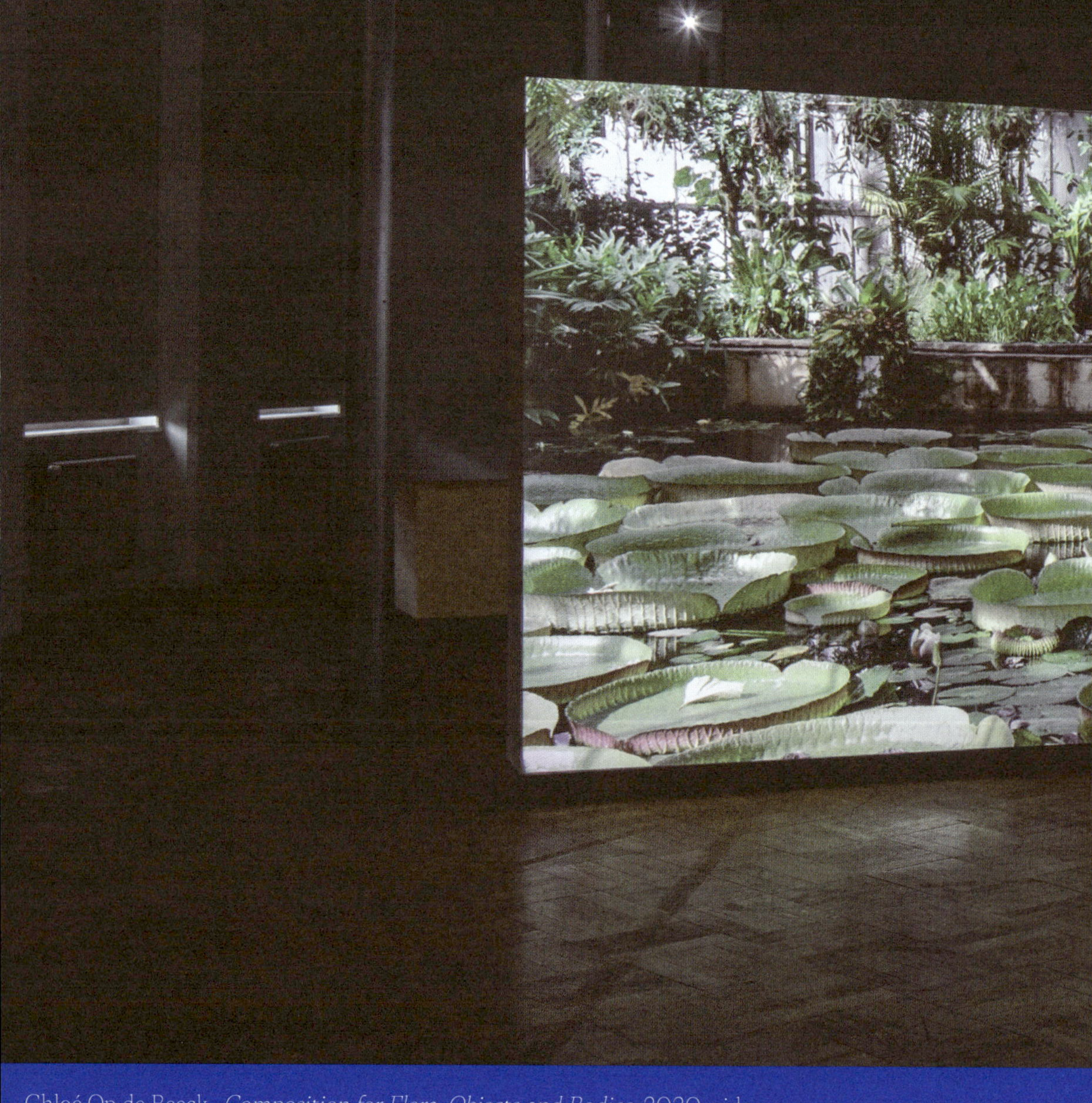

Chloé Op de Beeck, *Composition for Flora, Objects and Bodies.* 2020, video.
© Kristof Vrancken

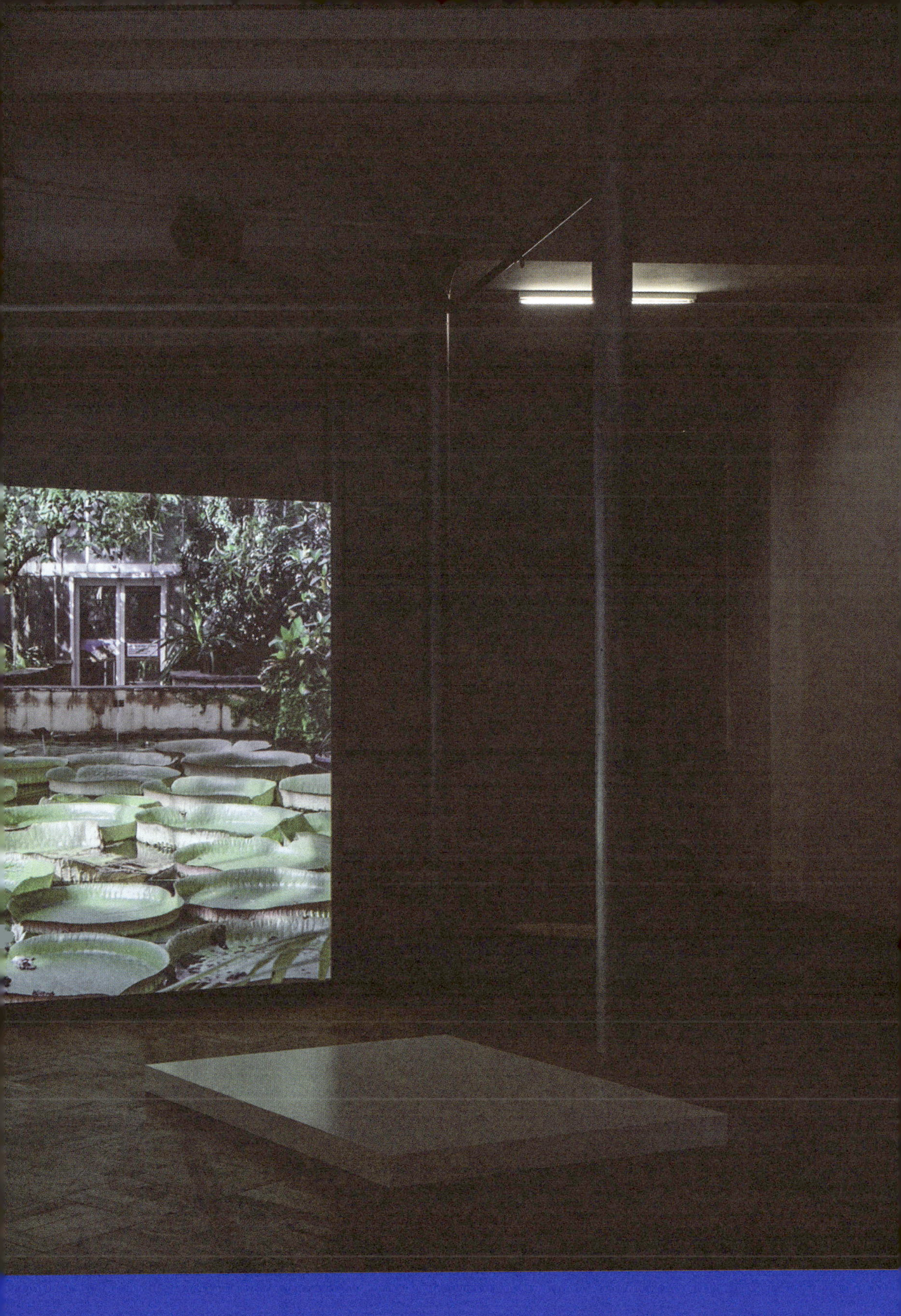

Let me make some responses to your questions you set out below.

---------- Original Message ----------
From: ChLoé
To: "John C. Welchman"
Subject: conversation
Date: Sun, Apr 16, 2017 20:42:34 +0000 (UTC)

A Post-studio-visit Email Exchange with Chloé Op de Beeck

CODB: Dear John Welchman,

I'm very happy that you suggested that we write a question, remark, or statement to continue the conversation. Your visit was one of the most challenging so far and as always when I have a visitor, a lot of questions and ideas came up after you were gone. I have been thinking about your remarks on the exploitation of people and places and on voyeurism in my work.

I was wondering if you would also say I exploit people and places even if the images were not pictures or videos, but drawings or paintings.

Is voyeurism also possible in drawing, painting . . . (so in mediums besides video or photography)? Is voyeurism an essential element of photography?

JCW: I think these problems or issues are clearly more related to photographic and film practices because of the immediacy of these representations. Almost by definition, drawings and paintings and similar forms of representation are more mediated . . . by time, distance, material intervention, and many other factors. It is the arrival of a representation instantaneously, possibly covertly, and reasonably completely that poses a particular issue in this regard.

CODB: And can you talk about voyeurism if nothing is really happening?

JCW: Well, voyeurism can take place, I think, no matter what is happening, whether what is seen or 'spied on' is something dramatic or eventful, or whether it is just an everyday occurrence, like walking or waiting in the street. I do think that the term voyeurism needs always to be situational; that is, it matters what is being seen, when it is being seen, by whom it is being seen, whether it is being recorded or otherwise represented, and maybe most important of all, how what is 'taken' is then recirculated to a viewing public. The contingencies of this complex chain of events always determine the nature of an event or episode of voyeurism. In and of itself the term 'voyeurism' is relatively neutral. I mean, every day we all sit somewhere, or will stand somewhere and watch something or someone in the street, in a café, in a classroom—and most importantly these days from the neutral, disembodied perspective of the screen—our whole life is measured out by these kinds of encounters. So perhaps voyeurism is a kind of default position. I would still argue, however, that it is

seldom a neutral one. There are always positions, of power,
class, privilege, need, want, desire . . . and dozens of other
contingencies that motivate the spectacle of a visual trans-
action.

CODB (2025): When I reread the email I was transported back to
that unsettled feeling. You visited me relatively early during
my time at HISK. Those first months—meeting so many people,
hearing so many perspectives and opinions about my work—were
quite a confrontation. But one I deliberately sought and needed
in order to gain a deeper understanding of my practice, to
learn to communicate about it in words which I find suitable,
and to develop my work further. A search that's still ongoing.

Shortly after your visit, I planned a trip to Shanghai. The
reason to go there emerged from my interest in the metropolis
and the organization of immense cities where architecture seems
to exceed human dimensions. I wanted to be alone in a place
where I don't understand anything of the language and where
signs are an abstraction.

However, after your visit, I began to question the relevance
of this trip. Upon arrival, I was wandering around the city and
felt paralyzed. I was unable to film anything, haunted by the
thought of me exploiting the place and the people. How could I
make images there and avoid that? Is it possible to engage with
an unfamiliar environment without objectifying it? Am I allowed
to be there?

These questions remain relevant and still stay with me. What
is my position as a maker? How can I capture my observations—my
way of seeing—without exploiting people and places? I believe
it's important to keep these questions in mind.

Eventually, I began filming, making sure I was always visible
while doing so. On several occasions, passersby would come and
stand next to me, curious about what I was capturing. They'd
look at the screen of the camera to see what was happening in
the frame.

Sometimes they wanted to start a conversation, but often we
simply looked together in silence. I remember a moment when it
felt like the people in front of the camera were somehow moving
with me, as if we were part of the same choreography. They
seemed to move as if they were following some unspoken direction. They were aware of me, acknowledged the camera, and yet
continued as if part of a quiet performance. It became a kind

of dance with me, the camera, and them.

Back in Belgium, I attempted to edit the material, but in the end–apart from a video of a turtle in a bucket–I decided not to use any of the footage.Instead, I made a video composed solely of text, shown as subtitles.

This makes me think of the photographer Garry Winogrand, who left behind thousands of undeveloped rolls of film. Perhaps, for him, the act of photographing was more important than the act of showing. It raises the question of whether the acts of image-making hold value independent of dissemination.

I think I can relate to Winogrand's urge to make images without the need even to work with them afterwards, at least to some degree: maybe I'm less concerned about producing art objects than with initiating a dialogue–with the world, with others, with myself. An attitude where life and art coincide.

Nonetheless, the desire for a viewer's presence and a shared moment of reflection remains significant to me.

CODB: Do you think that what I do is immoral? And do you think an artist should be moral?

JCW: I wouldn't want to say that your work, or indeed anyone's work, necessarily, was immoral, at least not without a very considered response. But work like yours raises questions of 'morality' precisely because its contexts involve the power and some of the many other positions I just mentioned. The question, I feel, is yours really: what do you feel are the moral stakes of the situation that you produce, and its role as an 'artwork.' The vexed issue of whether art in general should be moral is a huge question of course, and one of the philosophers who has thought most about this is Theodor Adorno. He has numerous complex and intricate formulations addressing how the questions that art poses are related to various historical, social, and indeed ethical questions . . . though he believes quite passionately that art should not take on an instrumental role in the service or pursuit of moral solutions. It is for him the formal, material, subjective, historical nexus of relations caught up in the making and reception of art–especially its production in and through language–that fronts onto moral questions.

CODB: While I'm filming, I'm not thinking about being a voyeur. One might think the voyeurism in my work is an interesting aspect because it says something about the female gaze, about a female kind of voyeurism. It's a part of my work, but not something I deliberately search for.

JCW: I think the gender relations caught up knowingly or unwittingly in your work are important. It is a bit strange to me that you don't see your work as having points of commencement in voyeurism. Because to a certain extent you have, self-consciously, to hide yourself, you have to shoot from a certain distance where you probably can't be seen (at least in some situations); and what you produce is of necessity completely different from what you might produce by filming or recording the same action close-up, by declaring your presence. In this regard, I think the boundaries between being covert or hidden at one extreme or completely declared at another are very interesting. I remember you spoke about one project, for which you were shooting I think in your own home, but in such a way that you were not hidden, but also somehow not really noticed or acknowledged. This gives rise to a situation that is intriguing and challenging; and I think one that you could work with very profitably.

CODB (2025): Yes, gender relations are very important. 2017 saw the rise of the #MeToo movement. Through exchanges with fellow artists at HISK I became increasingly aware of my identity as a woman and of things I thought were 'normal,' associated with being a woman. Moving through the world

alone is a distinctly different experience for a woman than
it is for a man. It made me think about the dominance of male
architecture and how the world is, both physically and conceptually, largely shaped by men. It led me to interview architects
and film inside and outside apartment buildings designed by
Renaat Braem (Antwerp) and Le Corbusier (Marseille). I wonder
what the world would be like if it were mainly designed and
run by women.

Before I started at HISK, I was already filming from less
hidden positions. During the past years I have deliberately
explored other methods to observe and make images, because I
was fed up with the conversation around voyeurism in my work.
It frequently overshadowed or stood in the way of being able
to talk about other things I wanted to explore and reflect on.

I also became more conscious of the tension between distance
and presence within my practice. I find this ambiguity an interesting characteristic. Observing 'inherently' implies a certain
detachment: removing yourself from a situation in a way. There
are, of course, other approaches to filming and photographing
where the artist is deeply involved in the moment, resulting
in a strong sense of personal presence, as with Nan Goldin, for
example. But my visual framing usually is more distant: I often
place myself in front of the subject or situation, creating an
image reminiscent of a stage or a theatrical setting, positio-
ning viewers as if they were witnessing a composed, staged
event.

CODB: When I told you that I'm looking for something fundamental about existence, you asked me if drama isn't the biggest
part of life. Of course, you could say that. But maybe I didn't
use the right words to make it clear. I think my attitude to
the world is rather Beckettian. Quite empty or naked. In a way
I purge things. Everything we see is some kind of organization.
Staged. Behind that, there's an emptiness. A lot of things look
artificial to me. Constructions of (public) space, organization,
architecture, habits and how we move and behave in certain spaces, etc., we take these for granted, but I don't think they are
so invisible or undeclared.

JCW: I think I know what you are getting at; but from my point
of view things, actions, or whatever they might be, that have

not yet been enunciated don't necessarily stand in front of something naked or empty. What exactly are the 'potentials' that come before something or that might have made something else possible? These are surely in part the codes of life, the system through which we all make things happen . . . the system of language above all, but also gesture, deportment, body articulation, daily rituals, and what have you. From a Marxist point of view the structuring articulation of Western capitalist society is ideological, so an invisible but omnipresent system canalizes our volition . . . we could use the formula 'making seeming being.'

CODB (2025): Indeed, these codes of life that you refer to are precisely the kinds of constructs I'd like to question. Rather than seeing them as a given, realizing they are an agreement between people, a construction, often to create meaning. This has become more explicit in my work, though it is still quite tacit.

For instance, in *Ara realis irrealis* (2023, 15'34") I show images of parrots in captivity in a zoo, accompanied by a voice-over of a woman reading grammatical rules. When these two elements are combined their artificial mechanisms of comprehension and control are emphasized. The work also reflects on how animals are transformed into objects of entertainment (for us to look at). This is also present in *Composition for Flora, Objects and Bodies* (2020, STUK, Leuven), filmed in Plantentuin Meise (Botanical Garden of Meise), where plants from across the globe meet each other in a carefully controlled environment and nature becomes curated. It's also present in the idea of a fountain (*However*, 2020) where water becomes a performative element. Or in *Variations of Presence* (2021) where I wonder about public spaces as 'sights' of visual consumption or tourist attraction.

The work I'm currently developing may address these themes more directly than any of my work to date. It explores the regimen of beauty ideals and instructional guides for women on how to attain 'beauty.' Many of the ongoing questions in my work converge in this work: the tension between the natural and the artificial, systems of control, questions around canonization and the power of manuals.

CODB: You also mentioned that what I do is not really making an artwork. I just go somewhere to steal some images and put them together randomly and as I'm an artist I label it as an artwork (you said). But what I do is of course not as random as you maintained. There's a sincere desire to observe and to be present in the world. By waiting, questioning, and doubting, I try to capture moments where delusions become apparent and what appears to be self-evident is stripped of inhabiting . . . and habits.

JCW: I think what I meant to say was not that what you do is not 'art,' but that your means of making are deliberately attenuated in line with a by-now very well-established legacy of appropriation going back to Marcel Duchamp and before. This way of working, by definition, places a special premium and more emphasis on the reception of the work, so that how it is understood, taken up, positioned by its viewers is relatively more significant. The work and academic critique of Sherrie Levine are good examples of this.

CODB (2025): Could you elaborate on this?

I understand what you say and find it very interesting in relation to my work, but Sherrie Levine's approach seems rather different to me, as her practice primarily revolves around the appropriation of existing artworks.

Could you clarify your analysis and specify what conclusion you are drawing in relation to my work?

The viewer's position is indeed very significant in my work. It reminds me of what Elly Strik once said after encountering my work– that my particular attitude, combined with the 'stillness' of my work, faces onto existential self-questioning.

CODB: I do have some difficulty with your contention that you are attempting to document a situation in which 'delusions become apparent.'

JCW: Unless we understand this claim in the most general of terms (i.e., that we all have delusions pretty much all of the time), I'm not sure that I would now say that this is what your work either does or even sets out to do. Again, I feel that delusion needs to be specific rather than abstract: somebody is deluded about something. And in a way that is precisely what your work cannot show, that person X or person Y is deluded about the fact that her sister, brother, uncle, son, lover is going to show up . . . Of course, we cannot know anything about the specificity of the situation . . . how delusion is actually socially operative here. In fact, I would argue, we can't even be sure that there is delusion. It just looks like there might be. And we are reading that into a situation rather than reading it out from something that is known. This might be one of the creative problems in the address of your work, that it prompts speculation about motive, about details, about family or relationships or whatever–about which we know very little. This renders the subject in question socially abstract, and we become witnesses of a pantomime of gestures, a 'dumb show,' almost, that is overburdened by significations, guesses, speculations that can never be addressed without acts of reading-in. In this sense, the delusion is really that of the artist or of the viewer, and once again that is not an uninteresting point of view . . . perhaps more could be made of this?

CODB: Yesterday I read a poem by Fernando Pessoa about what we see in which he writes that what matters is knowing how to see, knowing how to see when it is obvious. He says that requires study, an apprenticeship in unlearning. It made me think of one of my favorite writers, Francis Ponge.

JCW: This idea of art's relation to 'unlearning' has many sides, of course—and some affiliated issues are explored in Jacques Rancière's *Le Maître ignorant* (The Ignorant Schoolmaster, 1987).[1] The positive aspect being the idea of outwitting custom, design, rote thinking, conformity, and the like. But I have to say, in light of this weekend's March for Science and the general rightist reaction against knowledge, learning, and facts, there is also something dangerous, even indulgent, in this line of thinking which can so easily be abused. What we need is more knowledge and better knowledge and better use of knowledge, perhaps . . . we need to learn more and to learn differently, but always to learn.

CODB (2025): That's also how I interpret the words in the poem of Pessoa. I guess what he's suggesting is, in fact, to learn to see differently. Unlearning is also a form of learning. Avoiding a lapse into habitual patterns, and evident or obvious assumptions; setting aside preconceived knowledge. Trying to see things from a different angle than how you've been taught.
   That's not an easy thing.

CODB: My approach might seem arbitrary, but I believe intuition and curiosity are very important. I usually follow something without knowing exactly where it will lead me. Some things end up in a claim that allows me to wait for a longer time or helps me to follow another path. For example, I started painting a year and a half ago. At first because I wanted to practice my eye even more by looking at things, now I think paintings might get incorporated in my work as well. Sometimes it's frustrating because it's not always as efficient or doesn't necessarily lead to a result, but the uncertainty is necessary to discover something we are truly curious to follow and explore.

JCW: I have nothing against intuition, spontaneity, experiment, uncertainty, and the rest of it. If you're an artist or writer you live with these things, or we should, every day. But in the end what we do cannot be surrendered to these constituencies. No great art is always or mostly confined to these parameters. For me, uncertainty is a given, it's something we deal with all the time, perhaps it's a place of beginning. Perhaps making art is to a large extent about offering a challenge to what is uncertain in the name of a new possibility?

CODB (2025): For you, certainty is a given. That counts for me as well and, indeed, it's a place of beginning. But I notice this is also a challenge. There seems to be a strong desire for certainty and control—something ideologies and religion can readily provide. I guess I mentioned intuition, because theory and making works of art often don't fit together. In fact, I feel there's often a friction between the two. Developing a body of work, making, producing, are different ways of thinking, using a different language. I remember the artist Bernhard Rüdiger giving a presentation in which he said that he only knew what a particular piece he made was about thirty years after creating it.

CODB: My email is starting to get a little bit too long (I assume), so I will end here. With one more question: Do you remember the first time when you experienced beauty and if so, when was that and how did it occur?

JCW: The first time is lost. It probably got confounded with inter-personal relations at the age of five or six. But having lived a very nomadic life as a young man, always in different places, never having a 'home' that I could arrange or even identify with . . . I was struck when I bought my first (and only) house how I had no knowledge of and little appreciation for the beauty of everyday objects. And this arrived for me very suddenly when I threw myself into understanding, appreciating, gathering objects that could go inside the house . . . ceramics, furniture, carpets, etc. I had never been much interested in design or the so-called applied arts, and then for a little while the beauty of these things and their infinite possibility was overwhelming.

1 Jacques Rancière, *Le Maître ignorant: Cinq leçons sur l'émancipation intellectuelle* (Paris: Fayard, 1987); trans. Kristin Ross as *The Ignorant Schoolmaster: Five Lessons in Intellectual Emancipation* (Stanford: Stanford University Press, 1991).

Lisa Wilkens, *oberfläche, zukunft / druck, immer*, 2017, two-color Risoprint on paper , 32 x 45 cm.
Edition of 30, each edition consists of 2 pages.
Edition Nr 4, Galerie Mitte, Bremen.

pressure, imprint, handshake, heave-ho
,   ,

again, once again, determination,
determine, voice, language, speak,
translate, value, added value, more, work,
act, effect, create, quality,
accomplished,   ,   ,
experience, recognize, know,
forget, can and must, trust, dare to
trust one's own eyes, motive, motivated,   .
self-motivation, grasp, touch, grasp,
hand, handle, action, negotiate   ,   .
                                                  ,

work, do, make, time, sense, free, always

        ,   ,   ,   .
            ,   ,   ,   ,
            .

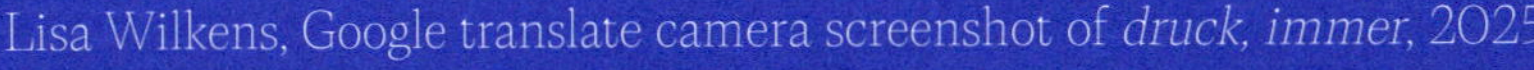

John C. Welchman (2025): This brief exchange is one of the shortest and, perhaps, the most informal, of the texts collected in the present volume. The exhibition to which Lisa Wilkens refers is Human Problems in Industry (Galerie Mitte, Bremen, Germany, May 13 to June 11, 2017; https://www.galeriemitte.eu/ausstellungen-veranstaltungen/ausstellungsarchiv/wilkens/). Its title derives from the eponymous book by Norah M. Davis (London: Nicholson & Watson, 1946), part of the series 'The New Democracy.' Wilkens chose six images from the book, drawing them in the style she had established using Chinese ink on large sheets of paper made in the former GDR (German Democratic Republic, also known as East Germany, 1949 to 1990). Predicated on her training in scientific illustration, and her formation in a politically active household, the project investigated the relations between manual labor and studio practice.

Shortly after this conversation the focus of our discussion in studio visits and follow-up emails turned to a new body of work that commenced in March 2018 with the loan and display in Wilkens's HISK studio of a work by Hanne Darboven, 7. Variante (1976), in connection with the HISK exhibition Trust Is Not a Mood, Barely an Emotion at ING Korenmarkt, Ghent (October 2017 to September 2018). Unfortunately, most of our animated exchanges on the political stakes of the visualization of language, women Conceptual artists, and commerce and compromise weren't saved.

From: Lisa Wilkens
To: John C. Welchman
Subject: Adorno und andere
Date: Thu, May 4, 2017 12:45:19 +0200

Dear John:

I hope you are well!

We met last month at HISK in Ghent, during the studio visits. Just a quick reminder, http://hisk.edu/mw/index.php/Lisa_Wilkens

An Email Exchange with Lisa Wilkens

It was good to hear from you about Adorno. Unfortunately, the close reading group was neither enlightening nor interesting, so I had given up on him.

And then I found his *Aesthetic Lectures* (1958-59) in a second-hand bookshop in Berlin and have been having a really good time reading them. Maybe it's because they're in German, but they seem to be much clearer and lighter. Apparently, *Aesthetic Theory* is based on those notes; but I found it almost impenetrable. I dare to say I understand now why you think he is still interesting to read today and my point below about the context between art theory and 'living' artists seems related.

I also found a book called *Bildtheorie zur Einfuehrung* (Image Theory, an Introduction) by Wolfram Pichler and Ralph Ubl. It's a very well-written little book. They refer to and recommend *The Domain of Images* (1999) by James Elkins and David Summer's *Real Spaces: World Art History and the Rise of Western Modernism* (2003). Do you know them, and if so, can you recommend them in the context of my work?

Another thing I would like to write to you about is a current experience I had with an art historian who wrote a text for a catalogue for an upcoming show in a small gallery in Bremen. I felt his text was not really suitable for the show as an introduction to my work and as a piece of art-historical writing it is quite pretentious and ranting. However, when I expressed my concerns about the text to the writer (I did not say it was pretentious or ranting, rather I said it had a different focus and tone in relation to how I think about the work).

In his opinion, the work of art does not belong to me as soon as I share it with the public and therefore is open unreservedly, to be examined and evaluated. And unless I can 'prove' that there are factual errors in the text, I can't declare it unfit for purpose.

I have a feeling this is a symptomatic situation . . . and I have heard similar things from colleagues and mentors, including in the recent Adorno reading group.

I thought the art historian's comments were rather crude (science = objectivity = truth … in German it is called *Kunstwissenschaft*) . . . and also somewhat patronizing, even an abuse of power.

Now my question: Is this how it works??? And if so, what options do I (really) have to respond? Or should I just let it happen and hope that whoever looks at the work develops their own thoughts?

It would be great to hear your thoughts on these points.

And if you would ever come back and do a master class or seminar on Adorno, I would be very happy!

For now, best wishes,

Lisa

+++

Hi Lisa:

On Adorno, it's great that you found the aesthetic lectures . . . I'm not sure that these are translated into English.[1] In any event I haven't read them thoroughly but do recall that they are both more lucid if in the end more preparatory and provisional than the somewhat over-articulated *Aesthetic Theory*, published in German in 1970, the year after Adorno died.

About the references to Elkins's *The Domain of Images* and Summer's *Real Spaces* . . . I'm not sure how useful these would be for you. The former argues for the expansion of our understanding of the image beyond the conventional purview of the art object and generic delimitations of art-historical discourse. The latter also turns away from the traditional formal and iconographical constructs of art history, but in order to articulate what Summers refers to as a 'post-formalist' mode of analysis that can accommodate a wide range of global visual practices (rather than just the Western canon).

Real Spaces, in particular, has an orientation that is somewhat antithetical to my own. As with much of the discourse on aesthetics, the shapes, patterns, and structures–and to a certain extent the symbolic organization–of art practice is elevated above its contexts, contingencies, and resonant specificity. What results is an over-generalized view of the signification of art objects, or images–which has always been the central problem of aesthetics or aesthetic theory. It's also an issue with Adorno, who grapples with the question: Can there be a wide-angle, generalized category of 'art' that is sustained by almost universalizing-type reflection? I have recently written an article on this problem, focusing on Adorno's relation to twentieth-century and contemporary (to him) art practices. To rehearse just one aspect of the situation I have described, I take issue with the ways that Adorno investigates, often symptomatically, the work of Pablo Picasso.[2] For a start, we are not sure to which 'Picasso' the philosopher's generalized mentions refer. Is it the Picasso of the so-called 'Blue' or 'Rose' periods, or the artist who, alongside Georges Braque, generated the revolutionary visual styles of analytic and then synthetic Cubism between 1909 and around 1915; is it to Picasso's fattened-up 'neo-classicism' of the post–World War I years, to the 'weeping women' of the later 1930s, or to the welded metal sculptures made in collaboration with Julio González beginning in the late 1920s? Clearly all of Adorno's Picassos do not embrace the political turn manifest in *Guernica* (1937), including the Picasso who threw in his lot with Communism between the mid-1940s and 1953. And how are all these 'earlier' Picassos, including 'the art movements that converged temporarily in Picasso' and 'took up the theme of antiquity'[3] aligned with the artist's later work, which was locked into a compulsive dialogue with the paintings of Diego Velázquez (notably in the Las Meninas series of fifty-eight paintings made in 1957), Edouard Manet (in a series of drawings and paintings from 1954 to 1970), and other artists? This is just prefatory to a discussion about 'proper name' art history, monography, structural and formal analyses, and above all–using Adorno's complicated notion of *methexis*–about art's relation to language. These concerns give on to what I refer to as a 'relational inner sanctum at the heart of Adorno's aesthetics from which art's complexly recursive relations with key operating concepts are (enigmatically) brokered.'[4]

Yes, it would be nice to do something at HISK on key philosophical
ideas in the twentieth century and how they were related to contemporary art. Maybe I'll suggest a lecture on Adorno or on Walter
Benjamin next time I come. I teach seminars on their writings at
the University of California.

The problem with the catalogue text that you describe, is, I have
to say, unfortunately, very common, especially for artists at the
beginning of their careers when they have no or little power over
galleries and publications. Sometimes the reverse happens, when a
powerful artist takes over all aspects of a publication including
editing and changing the text . . . which can be equally problem-
atic. There is not much you can do in a situation like this to be
honest apart from through diplomacy . . . I would work with the
gallery or whoever your best contact is around the exhibition and
see if you could get them to ask the author to open up another
space in the essay or make some changes. It's always better if
these requests come from the commissioning entity, whether a
gallery, gallery director, or a publisher, etc. The minute these
issues become confrontational or a matter of peoples' pride or
feelings getting hurt one way or the other they become almost
impossible. Young writers tend to be much more defensive about
their work and making any changes or modifications in dialogue
with an artist (at least this is generally the case). Frankly, when
I was younger, I was also prone to be annoyed or indignant if
somebody wanted a change that I didn't agree with or understand.

It is true, of course, that critics commissioned to write about an
exhibition or an artist should have the freedom to express themselves as they see fit; so the real issue here is the nature of
the commission and the intelligence and sensitivity that needs to
be brought to bear in order find the right kind of writer to pair
with a particular artist. But I think there is a category difference between a text written for an exhibition catalogue which
should be expected to feature some form of dialogue and exchange
with the artist and is not purposed to be outside or 'objective'
critique, or at least not only this . . . and a journal or magazine article in which the author is commenting or critiquing from
a more 'third party' point of view about an artist, a body of
work, or an art-related issue.

Hope this is helpful and that you get the catalogue matter
resolved as satisfactorily as possible.

Best,

John

1. Adorno's 1958 - 59 lectures were published in English some six months after our email exchange: Theodor W. Adorno, *Aesthetics: 1958/59*, ed. Eberhard Ortland, trans. Wieland Hoban (London: Polity, 2017).

2. John C. Welchman, 'Names, Écriture and Enigma: Adorno on Art as Writing,' *Zeitschrift für Ästhetik und allgemeine Kunstwissenschaft* (Hamburg: Meiner Verlag, 2017), vol. 62, no. 1, 2017, pp. 57-76. The essay was originally presented as a plenary address at the conference Global Adorno in Amsterdam (March 2015).

3. Theodor Adorno, *Aesthetic Theory*, ed. Gretel Adorno and Rolf Tiedemann, trans. Robert Hullot-Kentor, (Minneapolis: University of Minnesota Press, 1997), p. 298.

4. Welchman, 'Names, Écriture and Enigma: Adorno on Art as Writing,' p. 69.

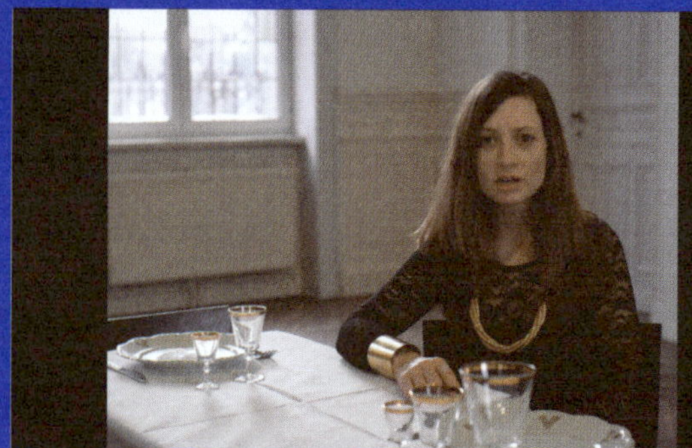

2016_LeBanquet_DialogueExcerpt1

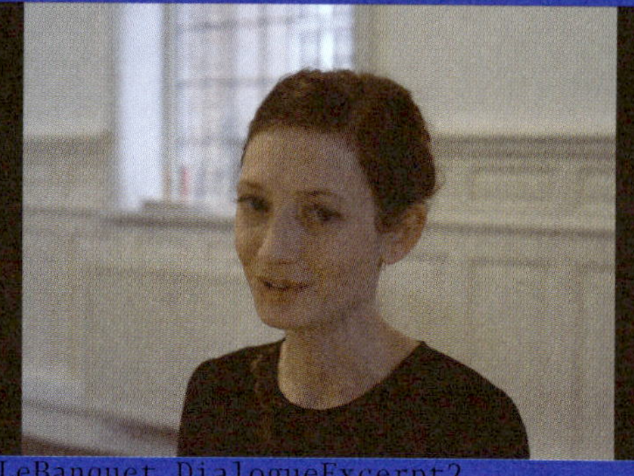

2016_LeBanquet_DialogueExcerpt2

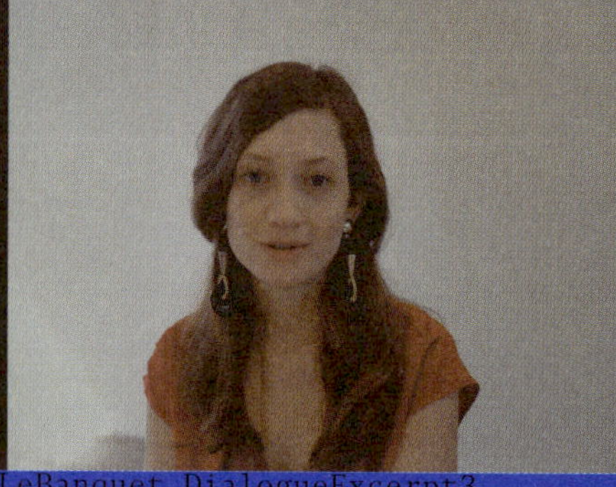

2016_LeBanquet_DialogueExcerpt3

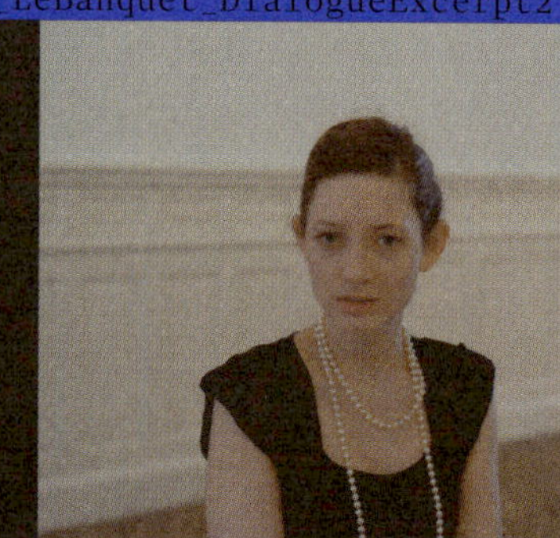

2016_LeBanquet_DialogueExcerpt4

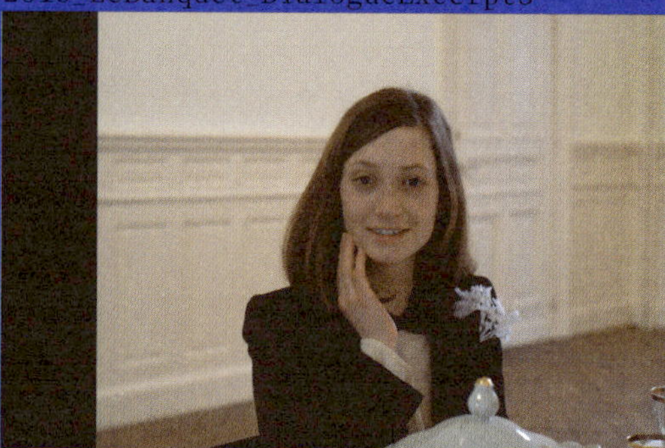

2016_LeBanquet_DialogueExcerpt5

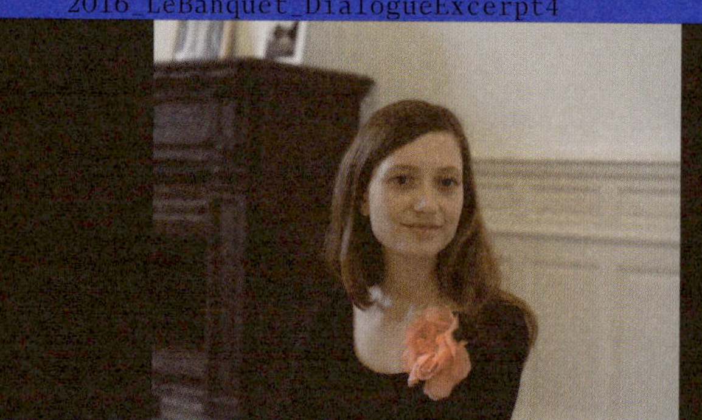

2016_LeBanquet_DialogueExcerpt6

Ariane Loze, *Impotence*, 2017, HD video projection with sound, color © Ariane Loze.
Courtesy of the artist and Galerie Michel Rein Paris | Brussels

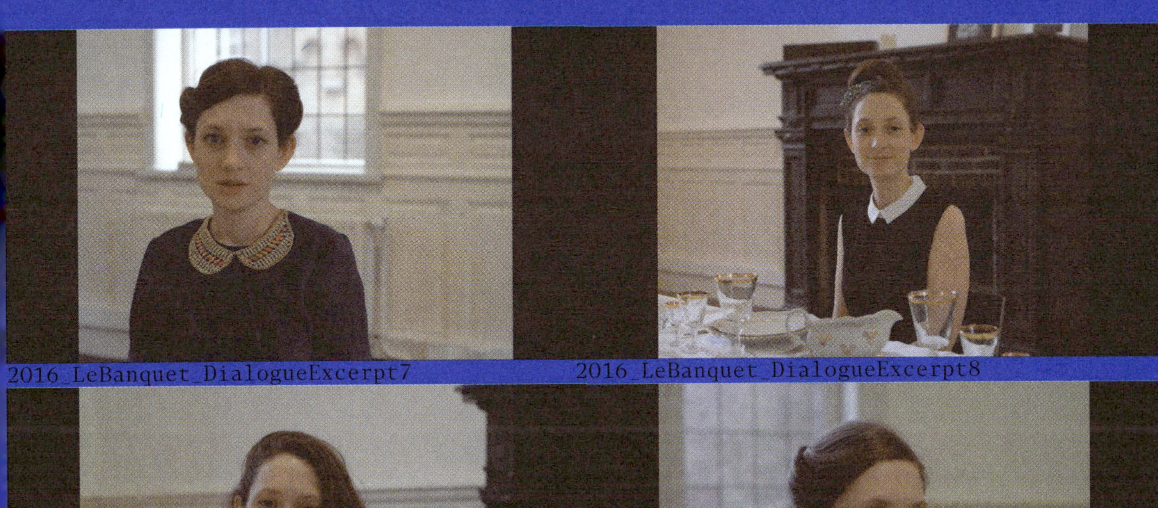

2016_LeBanquet_DialogueExcerpt7 2016_LeBanquet_DialogueExcerpt8

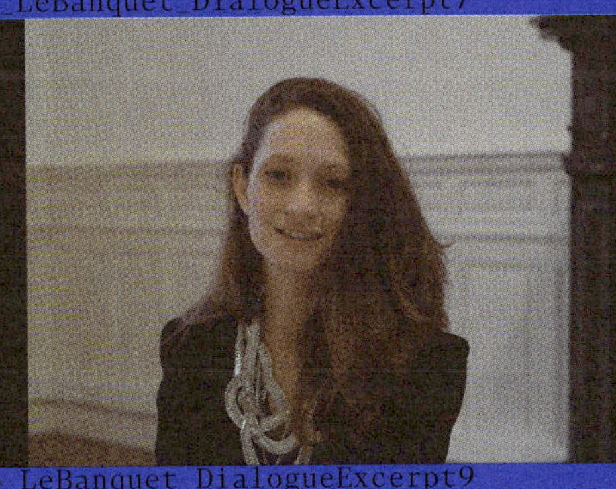
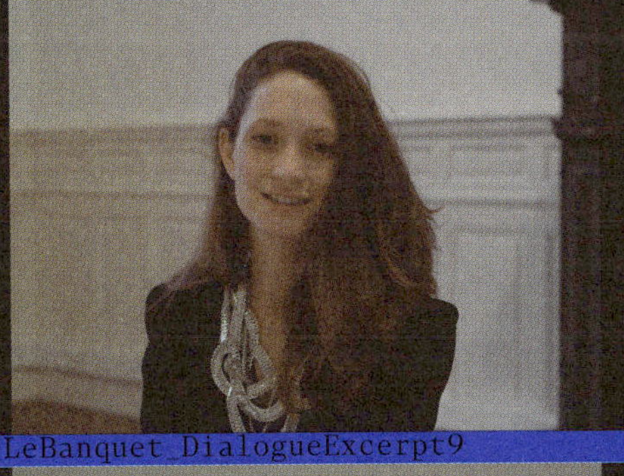
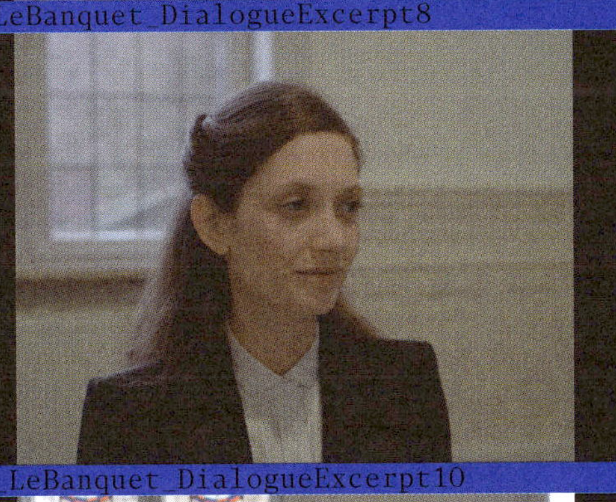

2016_LeBanquet_DialogueExcerpt9 2016_LeBanquet_DialogueExcerpt10

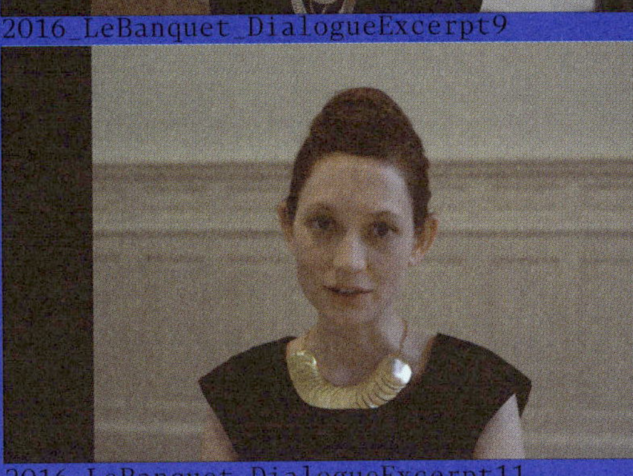
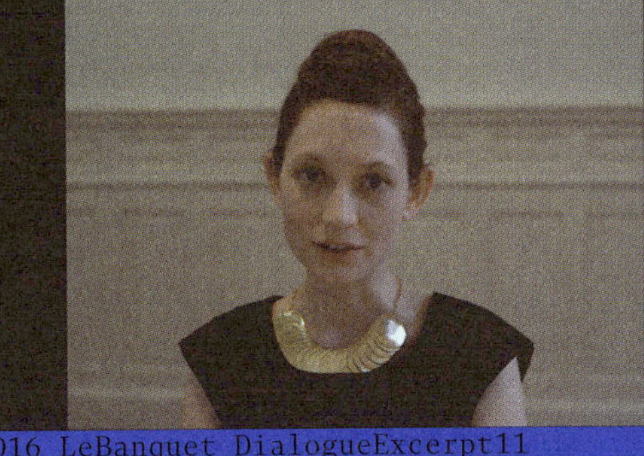
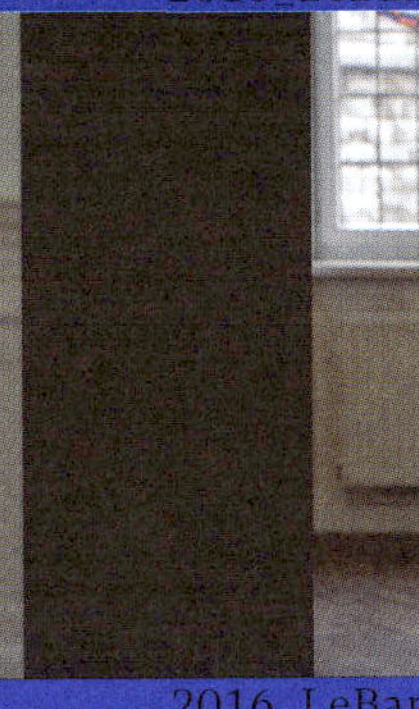
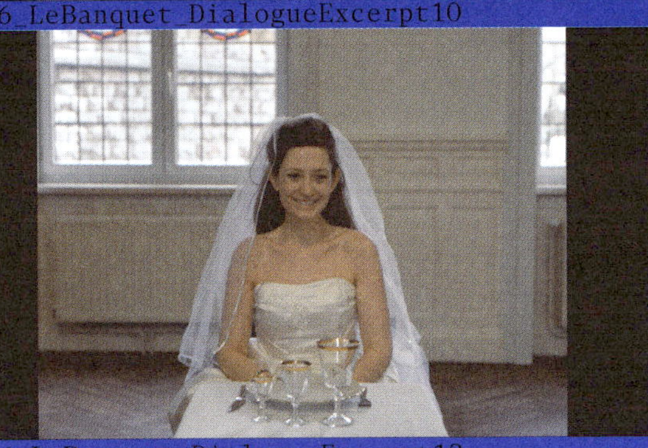

2016_LeBanquet_DialogueExcerpt11 2016_LeBanquet_DialogueExcerpt12

John C. Welchman (2025): This essay was commissioned, discussed, and written in the later summer and fall, 2017, and published in the catalogue for Trust in the Unexpected, Ambtswoning Gouverneur (The Governor's Mansion), Ghent, part of the annual exhibition of HISK laureates (October 14 to December 3, 2017).

During the first decade of her career the films of Ariane Loze have offered an extraordinarily concentrated focus on the dialectic between multiplicity and singularity, mobilizing her own corporeal performativity as a shifting envelope in which postures, gestures, manners, and appearances were locked in an uncanny form of recursive sociality. Looking back on this history from a moment in which Loze has dared to break with the parameters that situated her as an artist, we can see that her work—animated by serial self-reference and defined by processes summarized under the heading 'Movies on my own' (MÔWN)—was engaged in the costruction of and, as is now apparent, passage through its own version of the mirror stage.

These films produced exquisite moments of projective adjudication punctuated by the gestural intonation of a serial self. But there is a sense in which they finally gave rise to a kind of social suffocation which pointed to and put into crisis modes of reckoning outside the referential circularity to which they were almost exhaustively committed. The formations of class, gender, and other identities that Loze's films interrogated with such subtlety, mediation, and ironic diminuendo finally became modes of entrapment, or at least predicates from which the artist felt that that she could not escape.

Loze's riposte attempts to redirect her leporello of selves by removing their camouflage in the bourgeois milieu that spawned and nurtured them, all the trans-corporeal supplements over which she had such a secure command: costume, accessories, make-up, propitious props, and a remorseless and inimical mise-en-scène. What she is striving for is, surely, a latter-day variant of the forms of dispute with realism and naturalism on which the strategic reductions of modernist theater were predicated, from Pirandello and Brecht to Beckett. Like them she is putting into

Mown-Down: The Recent Videos of Ariane Loze

realization as Guy Debord put it that 'the spectacle's estrangement from the acting subject is expressed by the fact that the individual's gestures are no longer his [sic] own.'[1] Relinquishing this ownership is especially hard when it is funded by an exotic plurality of selves.

Within the turn now in progress, *The Banquet* (2016) is key. Here, around a dinner table set with an elaborate service, Loze interrogated a defining mantra of the millennial generation, 'I need time for myself,' realizing in the process that to refer social time back to the self, engendered an unhealthy 'refusal of the common.' In *Impotence* (2017), therefore, the artist seeks out a kind of reparation, using a calculus of 'anonymity' to conjure and reformat the effects of alienation and allegorical abstraction pursued in the socially conscious theater of the mid-twentieth century. Her aim is to bear witness to change rather than repetition or insinuation; to shift the terrain of multiplicity from the comfort zone of immersive critique to an operating system in which social and subjective modification is only possible in struggle; and to stage the risk of direct encounter with a consciousness that thinks and contends with the political.

This turn is brave and defining; for none of this, of course, is ever guaranteed.

[1]. Guy Debord, *The Society of the Spectacle*, trans. Ken Knabb (Canberra: Treason Press, 2002), thesis 30.

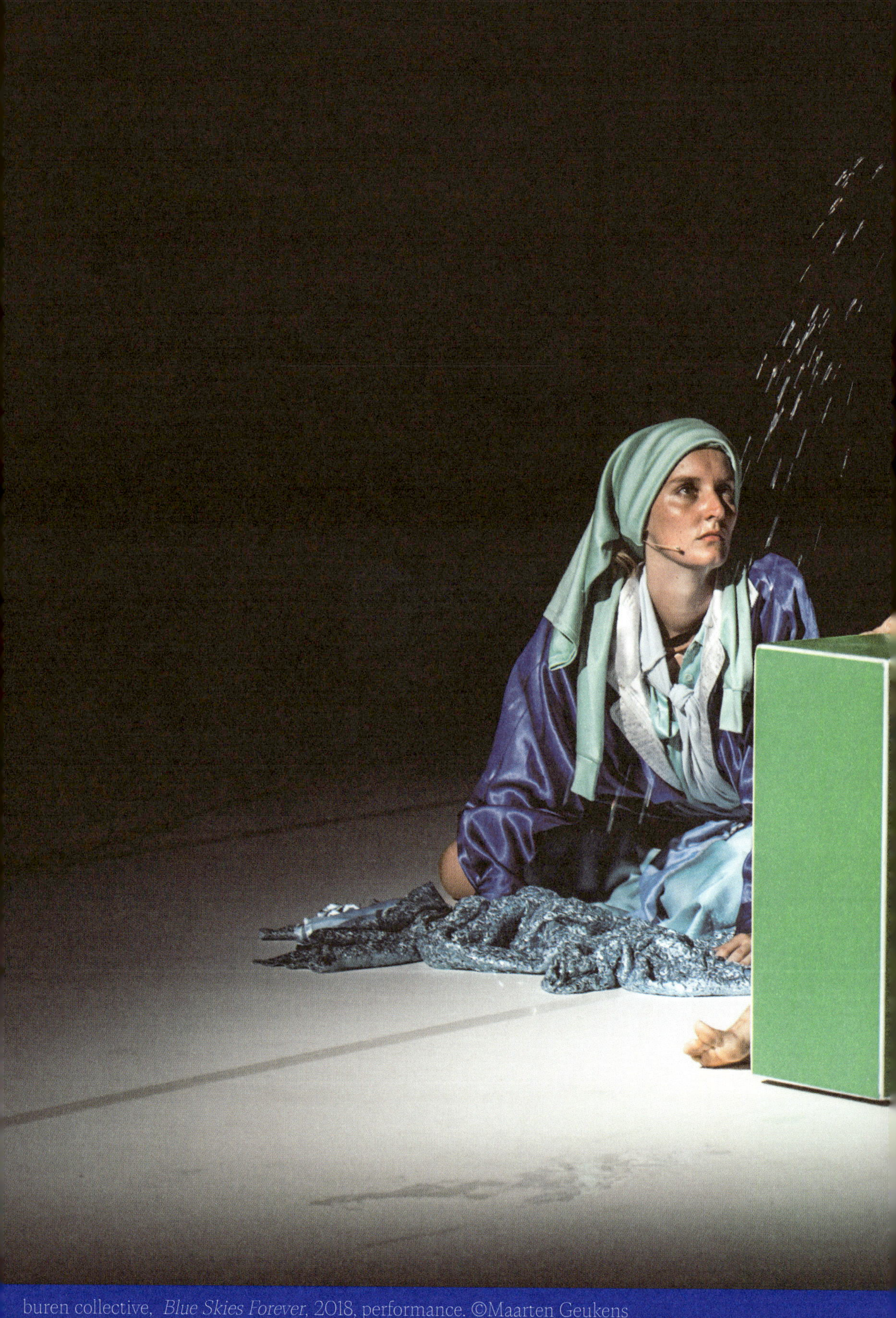

buren collective, *Blue Skies Forever*, 2018, performance. ©Maarten Geukens

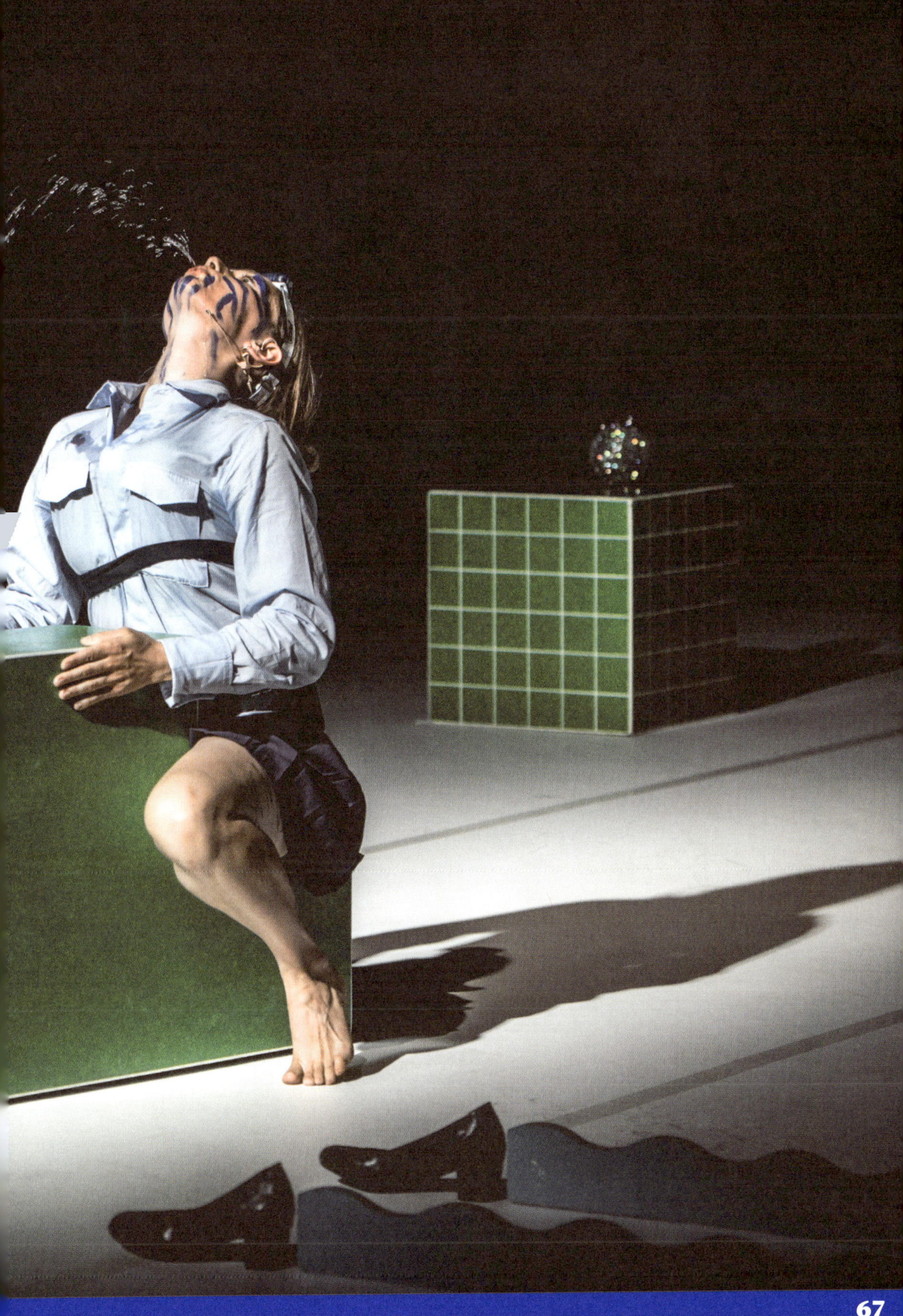

John C. Welchman (2025): *This essay was commissioned, discussed and written in the later summer and fall, 2017, and published in the catalogue for* Trust Is Not a Mood, Barely an Emotion, *ING Ghent (Kouter, 173), Belgium, an exhibition of work by HISK participants curated by Elena Sorokina (October 5, 2017 to September 25, 2018).*

Blue Skies Forever (2017), still a work-in-progress at this writing, began its life as an appropriative dialogue with another appropriation as buren duo Oshin Albrecht and Melissa Mabesoone took stock of the relation between Beyoncé's music video *Hold Up* (2016) and *Ever Is over All*, a two-channel video with overlapping projections on adjacent walls by the Swiss artist Pipilotti Rist, made some two decades earlier in 1997. If the post-MTV video for Beyoncé's anthem is played out in angry gestures that might reinforce aspects of female dependency, the chromatically saturated and riotously mannered provocation of Rist's 'original' holds the 'natural' order and social expectation to a ransom of joyously delinquent spontaneity. A young woman in a blue dress and red shoes saunters along a Zurich street smashing car windows with a giant long-stemmed flower, resembling those in the appositional video which spills onto the urban narrative and is referred to by the artist as 'clitoric.' Rist herself seems to give permission for the kind of projective imagination ventured by buren when she suggests that *Ever Is over All* delivers an exhilarating sense of possibility, that it is a kind of 'rehearsal for a feature' in which one could 'go out and dare a bit more.'[1]

Buren converts the potential feature into one of their signature installation-cum-performances and ups the ante on the admonition to do more by doubling down on its allegorical potential. They focus, in particular, on the implications of Rist's hanging denouement, a cannily supercharged moment in which a female police officer strolls past the flower-wielding woman in full view of her extralegal caprice and exchanges with her a subtly flagrant nod and smile, redolent of camaraderie and complicity, though not quite reducible to either. Set alongside the figure of Dorothy–borrowed, like Rist's flower-girl, from MGM's Technicolor musical fantasy *The Wizard of Oz* (1939)–the authority figure or 'Officer' is amplified into a

Blue Skies Forever: buren

leitmotif of *Blue Skies Forever*, where it is subject to a fusillade of metaphoric extensions that are almost Ovid-like in their perfervid transmutation. Liberated by the sense that there may be 'no "outside" calling [us] to order,' buren uses costumes, permutational sets, and morphing soundscapes in concert with indicating objects and symbolic gestures to unravel stereotypes of discipline, desire, and dissipation.

The duo's hectic accumulation of metamorphic two-steps stakes out a vertiginous arena in which issues, concepts, historical personae, and critical revisionism are read between the lines of a prop-denominated, shape-shifting performance. Much in all this converges on experiences and representations of gender, including questions around the codes and effects of female self-presentation routed through dress, intonation, and role-playing. Buren's categories, already imagined as strategically elastic, are accelerated by the plastic, almost molten, valences of the production. Thus, in addition to glimpses of the psychological mythography of Cecilia Condit, the DIY, feminist punk of riot grrrl, or the extended compositions of Robert Ashley, buren also alludes to the creative, world-conjuring mantras of Minecraft—in both its physical denomination as 'the building blocks of a developing mind' and the construction of virtual worlds 'without boundaries.'

Pushing ever further, they take on the conceptual iconography of avant-garde kingpin Marcel Duchamp, especially the two-pane structure of *La mariée mise à nu par ses célibataires, même* (The Bride Stripped Bare by Her Bachelors, Even) (1915–23). But rather than antagonizing a traditional binary logic between female (bride) and male (bachelor)— the latter associated with a graphic regimen of nine 'malic molds' representing masculine professions and dominated by three arms of the law (gendarme, cavalry soldier [cuirassier], policeman)—buren's coupled formations pose both authority and becoming as female, while challenging the stability of both.

1. Pipilotti Rist interviewed by Patricia Bickers, Tate Modern, London, June 6, 2009; available at http://www.tate.org.uk/context-comment/video/pipilotti-rist-talking-art.

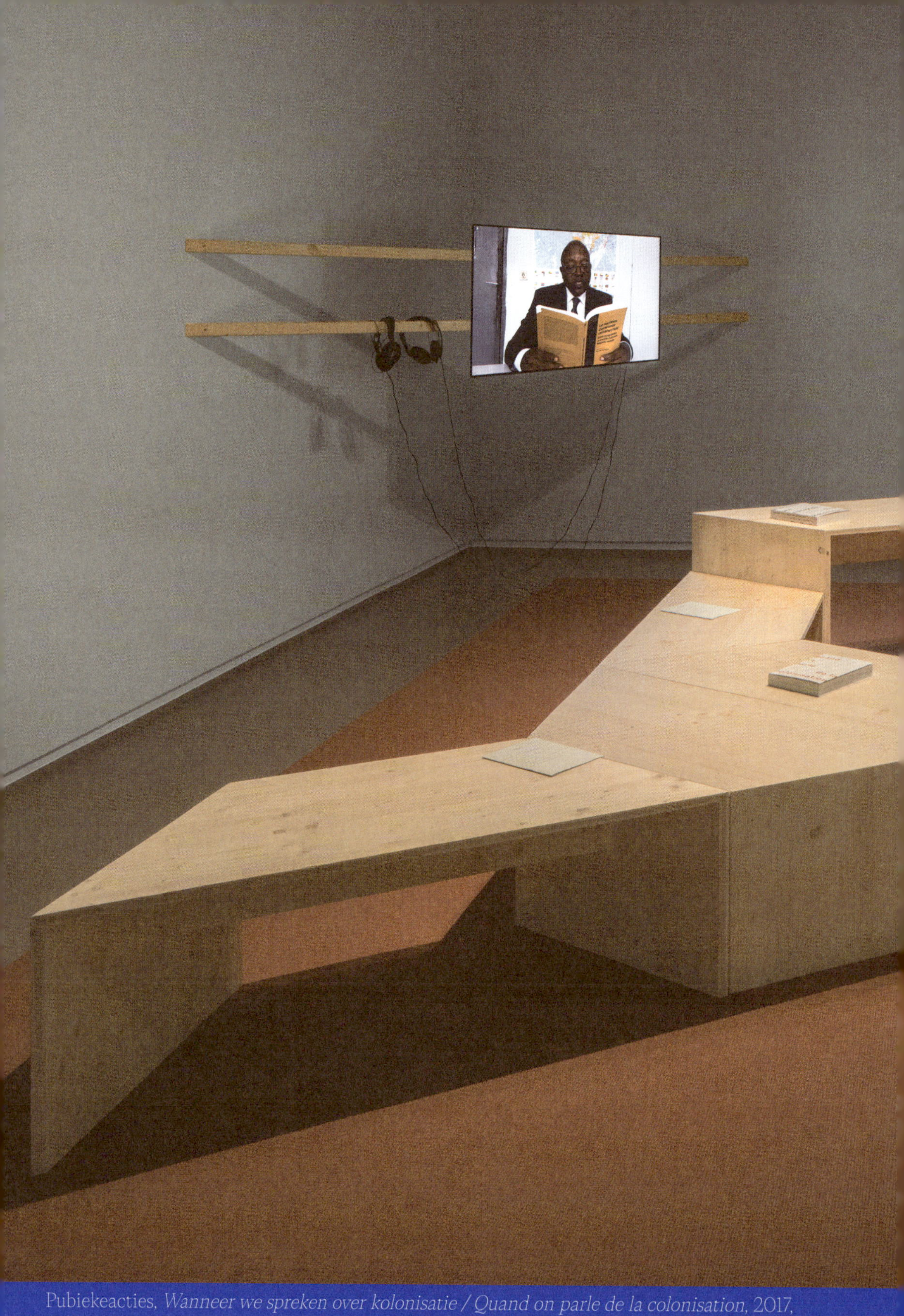

Pubiekeacties, *Wanneer we spreken over kolonisatie / Quand on parle de la colonisation*, 2017, Publicity Image, modular installation with text, video, and conversation.

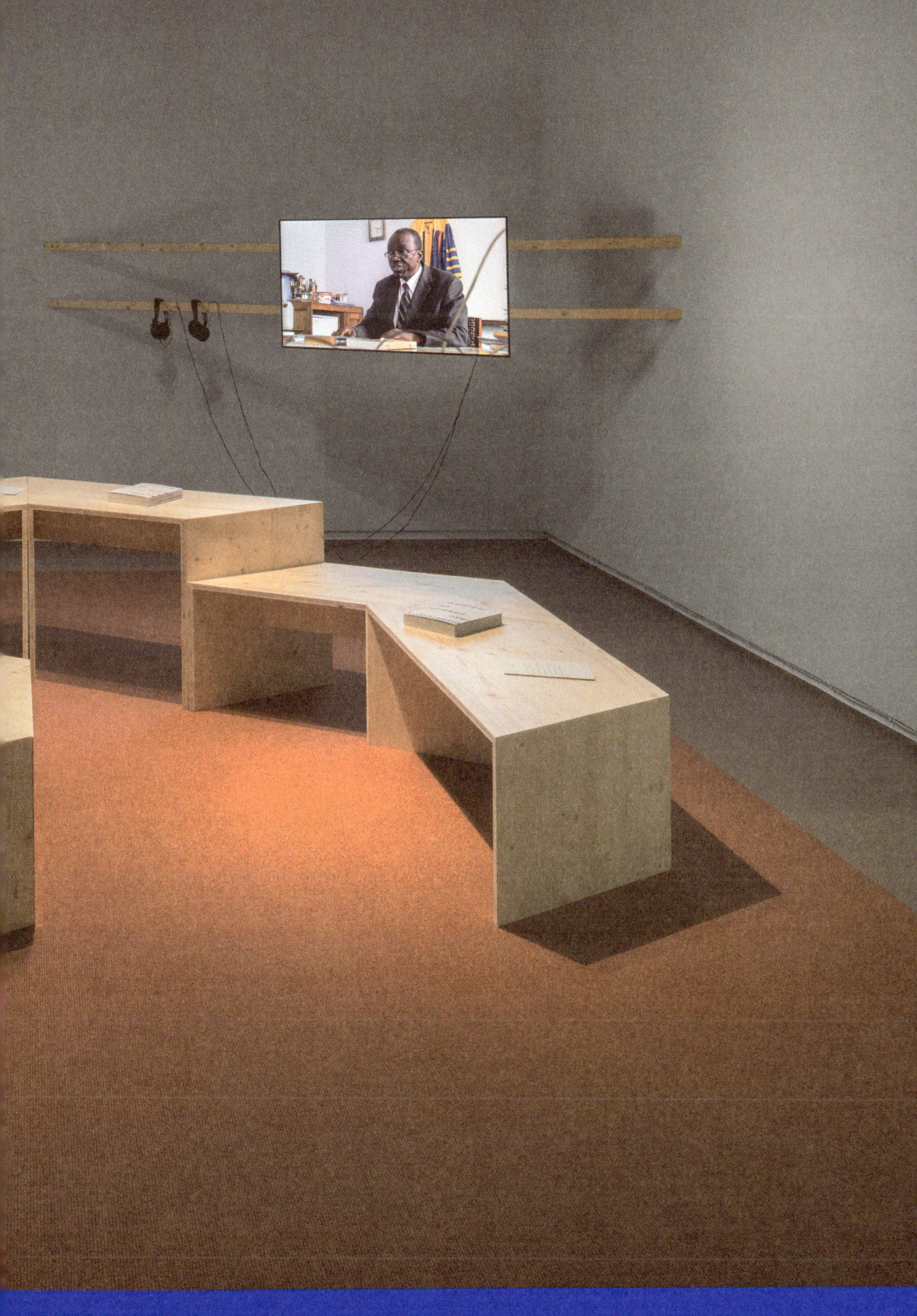

John C. Welchman (2025): *Based on conversations and follow-up with the collaborative duo Vesna Faassen & Lukas Verdijk, this essay was published in the catalogue for the exhibition of work by HISK participants* The Grid and the Cloud: How to Connect, *curated by Elena Sorokina, on the fourth floor of the Vanderborght Building, Schildknaapstraat 50-5 rue de l'Ecuyer, Brussels (November 23 to December 17, 2017). The exhibition also featured work by buren, Ella de Burca, Kasper De Vos, Aslan Gaisumov, Elias Ghekiere, Pepa Ivanova, Ola Lanko, Rebekka Löffler, Ariane Loze, William Ludwig Lutgens, Cadina Navarro, and Jonathen Paepens.*[1]

This brief essay is the most 'critical' in the current volume. I felt that what Vesna and Lukas needed most as they advanced their ambitious project was a reminder of the stakes and risks of their venture; and of the many issues and problems that they should in good faith confront, including but not limited to their own histories, identities, positions—and limitations. I wanted them to ask candid questions about what they could, might, and also couldn't do; to situate their research as fully as possible in the tangled discourses of post- and decolonial studies; and to interrogate the moral underpinings of their endeavor.

Faassen & Verdijk configured the project with artist Laura Nsengiyumva, who invited Afro-Belgian readers to make handwritten notes in the book Wanneer we spreken over kolonisatie / Quand on parle de la colonisation. *The project was also developed as an installation in which they organized book clubs and talks (https://faassen-verdijk.com/wwsok-book-club/). A related audiovisual installation and book publication,* Being Imposed Upon, *addressing feminism and decolonization, was developed between 2018 and 2020 with the assistance of a committee of female Afro-Belgian activists, writers, and thinkers (Heleen Debeuckelaere, Gia Abrassart, Sabrine Ingabire, Anne WetsiMpoma, Modi Ntambwe, and Tracy Bibo-Tansia). See, https://faassen-verdijk.com/being-imposed-upon/ and the associated publication (Eindhoven, NL: Onomatopee Projects, 2020).*

It goes without saying that any bid to put a part of the traumatic history of modern Africa into representation by explicitly soliciting its own agency is fraught with peril and provocation. As acknowledged, somewhat at least, by the producers of this project, such an effort is built on flimsy stilts supported by a cloud of ignorance: the ignorance that arises from lack of research and study in and of the Congo; ignorance of the languages in which histories of the Congo might be written, including French; ignorance about the receptive

---

Out of Africa: on Vesna Faassen & Lukas Verdijk's Wanneer we spreken over kolonisatie / Quand on parle de la colonisation

scene of such histories in 'sophisticated,' post-colonial, academic
milieux in Belgium or the Netherlands–and of the debates they
might occasion; and ignorance of the university press-type publish-
ing and distribution and their attendant apparatuses–conferences,
symposia, reviews.

The point here, however, is that *Wanneer we spreken over kolonisatie / Quand on parle de la colonization* (When We Speak about Colonization) is explicitly ventured within an economy of absences predicated on the agonizing deficit of so much that has already gone
without saying: the fraudulent premises and misleading structures
that underwrote King Leopold II of Belgium's colonialist adventur-
ism in the 1860s and 70s; the unspeakable atrocities perpetrated
by the Force Publique in Leopold's Congo Free State in the later
nineteenth and early twentieth centuries; the underdevelopment and
overexploitation visited upon the region for the last hundred and
fifty years; the crisis of independence abetted by the extrajudi-
cial murder of the new nation's first prime minister, Patrice
Lumumba, in January 1961, just a few months after his accession;
and the shadow of all this that falls in the present as the Congo
remains one of the poorest and most vulnerable nations on earth,
its abundant 'natural resources' notwithstanding.

It was Lumumba who noted in a letter to his wife in 1960 that
when 'history will one day have its say it will not be the history
taught in the United Sates, Washington, Paris or Brussels . . .
but the history taught in the countries that have rid themselves
of colonialism and its puppets. Africa will write its own history,
and both north and south of the Sahara it will be a history full
of glory and dignity.'[2] The question before us is whether the tragedy, misrepresentation, and ignorance through which the recent history of the Democratic Republic of the Congo has been filtered,
can be mitigated, even if fractionally, by delivering back to a
Belgian public, more specifically to its Dutch-speaking community,
some part of that stirring narrative created from within to which
Lumumba pointed in hope and expectation.

Flying in the face of omnivorous ignorance, Vesna Faassen & Lukas
Verdijk have offered a reflex reaction–with drawn-out consequences–
to the unsettling contention in a 2011 article ('Congo in onze
navel' [Congo in Our Navel]) by Idesbald Goddeeris that there are

no books written by Congolese historians, educated and living in Congo, that have been translated and published in Flanders in the Dutch language.[3] They took it upon themselves to supply this lack, using a network of contacts to solicit essays and texts from scholars and writers in Congo.

Faassen & Verdijk have opted for an uncompromisingly pragmatic approach, caught somewhere, as they observe in their preface, 'between risk and trust,' that is strategically different from the more subtle, mediated, even refractive, methods that have characterized other recent art-world negotiations with Congo, including T. J. Demos's extended dialogue with what he terms the 'specters of colonialism in contemporary art.'[4] Perhaps it takes a certain kind of naivety to resurrect a measure of palpability for the demonized haunting that interrogates the rhetoric of justification for colonial crimes explored, for example, in Sven Augustijnen's *Spectres* (2011) or the ironic remedialism and almost desperate self-referentiality of Renzo Martens's *Episode III (Enjoy Poverty)* (2009), shot in Congo. Instead, we confront here a self-consciously flawed but somehow inevitable form of direct action. Read and see.

1. For a curatorial statement and discussion of the two terms elided in the exhibition title, *The Grid and the Cloud*, see https://www.e-flux.com/announcements/165644/the-grid-and-the-cloud-how-to-connect/#:~:text=The%20Grid%20and%20The%20Cloud%3A%20How%20to%20Connect.%20is%20conceived,threats%2C%20risks%20and%20collateral%20effects.

2. Patrice Lumumba, letter to Pauline Lumumba, in *Lumumba Speaks: The Speeches and Writings of Patrick Lumumba, 1958-61*, ed. Jean Van Lierde, trans. Helen R. Lane (Boston: Little, Brown and Company, 1972), pp. 422-43.

3. Idesbald Goddeeris, 'Congo in onze navel: de omgang met het koloniale verleden in België en zijn buurlanden' (Congo in Our Navel: Dealing with the Colonial Past in Belgium and its Neighbouring Countries), *Ons erfdeel* 54 (2011), no. 1, pp. 40-49.

4. See, T. J. Demos, *Return to the Postcolony: Specters of Colonialism in Contemporary Art* (Berlin: Sternberg, 2013).

John C. Welchman (2025): *This essay was commissioned by the Belenius Gallery, Stockholm, Sweden, for the catalogue of the two-person exhibition* The Man in the Moon: Adja Yunkers and Indrikis Gelzis *(February 22, to April 1, 2018). The show set paintings and collages by Adja Yunkers (b. Riga, 1900, d. New York, 1983) from the 1920s through the 1970s alongside recent wall sculptures by Gelzis made using square metal tubes, fabric, and furniture plates and titled for days of the week,* Monday, Tuesday, Wednesday. . . . *Responding to correspondence about this volume, Gelzis provided a brief text reflecting on the continuity of his work over the last seven years (below). He mentions* Night Flame *(2025), shown in the one-person exhibition* Water Day's Eye *at the Kim? Contemporary Art Centre (August 25 to October 8, 2023) and nominated for the Purvītis Prize 2025 at the Latvian National Museum of Art (April 12 to June 8, 2025).*

Indrikis Gelzis (2025): *I still have the same ten fingers, the only ones accountable for digging the same persistent hole. Nothing heroic, just repetition, insistence. The gestures repeat like a reflex, but the ground beneath them is no longer stable. Loyalty to materials is consistent—wire, surfaces, the skin of things; but life is different. It splits, accumulates, complicates. Form used to offer some sense of order, a rhythm to hold onto. Now it flickers, buckles, leans into its own instability. The structures I build are not certainties; yes, they are constructions of circumstance, like* Night Flame, *where the anatomy of a neck, through which words slip, meets the wild, unpredictable heat of a bonfire, in which they are lost to the flames. Your essay caught something right before things turned; an edge of articulation before things became messier, maybe truer. The digging doesn't stop, it just goes on with less performance, more necessity. Sometimes you hit something. Sometimes it caves in. Still, the same fingers.*

While starting out as an apprentice to Emile Nolde in the milieu of German Expressionism and finding himself some decades later at the epicenter of American Abstract Expressionism in New York in the 1950s, the fundamental commitment in the work of Adja Yunkers was always additive or supplemental rather than gestural.[1] He took up with layers, superimpositions, and folds, the manifest content of a technique predicated on accretion that while derived from, or simply most visible in, print-making and collage, was also characteristic of his work in oil, gouache, and pastel—especially after he came under the influence of the cutouts of Henri Matisse and color field painting,

Lucidity Is Rage: Adja Yunkers and Indrikis Gelzis

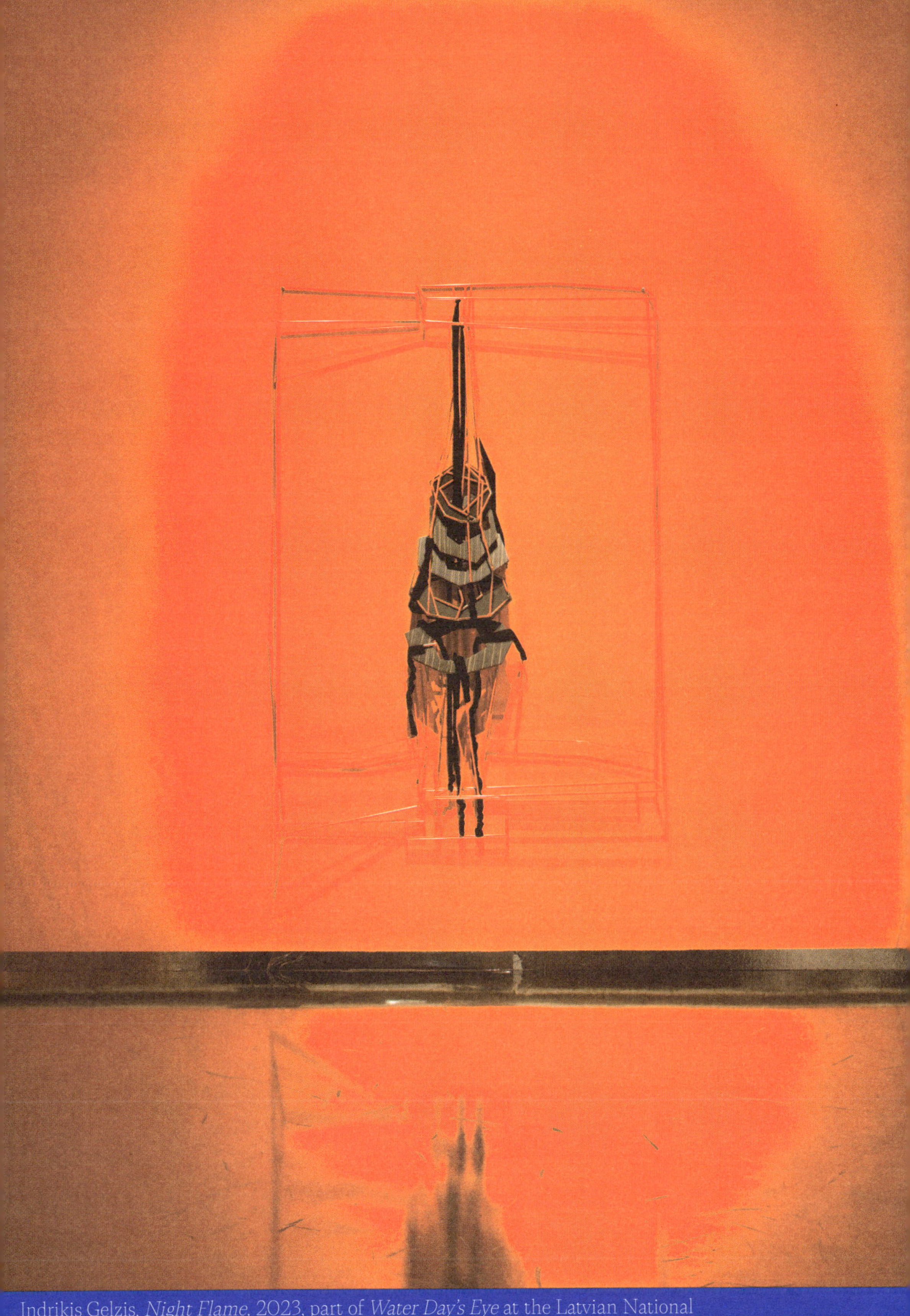

Indrikis Gelzis, *Night Flame*, 2023, part of *Water Day's Eye* at the Latvian National Museum of Art, included in the Purvitis Prize exhibition.

in the 1960s. The 'large lift ground plates' he etched for several days in acid in the mid-1970s at Styria Studio in New York are emblematic of this focus,[2] their scale and manipulability also suggesting–as does the present exhibition–how the logic of accumulation and juxtaposition might be framed in three rather than two dimensions.

Yunkers's work, I want to suggest, anticipates what Leo Steinberg proposed in 1968–borrowing his leading term from printing technology–as a new mode of artistic address organized around 'the flatbed picture plane' conceived as an accumulating 'receptor surface on which objects are scattered, on which data is entered, on which information may be received, printed, impressed.'[3] A review of an exhibition of works in pastel and tempera by Yunkers at the Fried gallery in 1957 makes these associations clear by pointing to the artist's multiple articulations of the surface, his 'layered horizontals' and his quest for a 'surface existence, through color, for his almost mechanical or automatic (or readymade) forms.'[4] Made a dozen or so years later–shortly after Steinberg framed his thoughts–the collage-based works in the current exhibition negotiate with the cutout logic of the flatbed proposition, even if they are not fully realized within this language. Heavy, roughly torn papers with ragged edges are posed on and over fields of acrylic paint, which sometimes finds its way back onto the collaged materials in the form of smudges and traces. Redolent of the figure-ground dialectic at the end of its hegemony, the 'stacking' and reformatting of reference in these works extends in several dimensions. In *White with Blue Stripe #X* (1969) and *Figure at the Seaside* (1969), similar compositions are diverted into different signifying economies, one formal, the other iconographic. *The Letter 'A'* (1969) refers directly to an alphabetic sign–actually splitting the letter into triangle and tripod forms, underscoring its makeup as a composite of two more elementary shapes. While another collage from 1971 is a 'sketch' for a print dedicated to Mark Rothko, who reflected more explicitly than any of the Abstract Expressionists on the question of how to articulate in layers. 'It occurs to me in our discussion of space,' he

suggested in the mid-1950s, 'that it would be profitable
to use pseudonyms which are more concrete in subjective
attributes as for example depth, for the experience of
depth is an experience of penetration into layers of
things more and more distant.'[5]

It is on the site of this challenging informational
orientation, provisional but emergent in the work of
Yunkers, that the relation to the sculptural practice
of the young Latvian artist Indrikis Gelzis–currently
living in New York City like his illustrious forebear–is
most apparent. For Gelzis engages with the formatting,
appearance, but also the social implications, of the
graphic organization of statistical data, so prevalent in
today's media and streetscapes. His new, wall-based sculptures develop a language using square metal tubing, swatches of fabric, and wooden plates in which the comportment of information is aggregated with suggestions of
modular domestic living and standardized workplace fur-
nishings. Here, the reorientation from vertical to horizontal articulated by Steinberg has in turn been overlaid by a striking conjugation of the locales in which
contemporary life is experienced: at home, at work, entered into, but also passed by.

The 'infogrammatical' organization of Gelzis's sculptures
adds another dimension to the innovative, spreading flat-
ness posited by Steinberg. For not only do these works
refuse to conform to either vertical or horizontal legi-
bility, but they also incorporate a new stratum of data-
based knowledge generally plotted out on the axes of a
graph. In other words, they service the space between the
defining parameters of up and down. Yet as with Rauschen-
berg's *Bed* (1955), the work that for Steinberg delivered
on his flatbed theory most insistently, Gelzis also attempts to embody as well as embed. His seemingly neutral
materials include the kind of fabrics used for covers and
upholstery, pointing us to the off-stage implications of

a remaindered action. In previous work these allusive scenes have included sexual (in the exhibition *Between the Sheets*) and workplace encounters, and references to conversation and exchange.

Like Steinberg, too, Gelzis is interested in the split between the artificial and the organic symbolized for the American by how 'the tilt of the picture plane from vertical to horizontal [is] expressive of the most radical shift in the subject matter of art, the shift from nature to culture.' But he presses this question further, suggesting a split between the experiential body and a data-processing head that is mirrored in the technique he employs. Building a virtual image using 3D modeling software, he waits for a certain moment of realization before reverting to effortful physical work 'welding, bending, grinding, burning . . . oiling, sewing.'[6] This interleaving of mental and physical, conceptual and practical circumstances, was also important for Yunkers, who somehow smuggled the implications of print-based work and material manipulation through the dénouement of gesturalism in 1950s New York. As he noted himself in what Dore Ashton called a 'rather technical description' of the monotype published in *Tiger's Eye*, 'free execution' was a 'distrustful no-man's land of shadow.'[7]

Gelzis's sculptures at the Belenius Gallery offer an innovative address to a theme as old as modern art itself: the experience of leisure. Looking beyond the confines of work or the probable privacy of a sexual encounter, he color-codes off-duty experience (things that transpire, as the Los Angeles artist Mike Kelley famously put it, after the working 'Day Is Done') by employing fabric in two basic hues both redolent of crepuscular or early morning light, the atmospheric brackets, to which Claude Monet also attended, that cordon off the temporality of normative, wage-earning labor.

Octavio Paz helps us to glimpse a final point of reconciliation –in constituencies of memory–between Yunker's shadow-shy layers and the corporeally inflected framework analysis of down-time reached for by Gelzis:

> memory weaves, unweaves the echoes:
> in the four corners of the box
> shadowless ladies play at hide-and-seek.[8]

1. I borrow the title of this brief essay from the first lines of 'Intermitencias del Oste (3)' a poem by Octavio Paz dedicated to Yunkers and his wife Dore Ashton: 'La limpidez . . . no es límpida: es una rabia;' *The Collected Poems of Octavio Paz, 1957-1987*, ed. and trans. Eliot Weinberger (New York: New Directions, 1991), p. 224. For an account of the life and work of Yunkers, who was born in Riga (Livonia) in 1900, studied in Petrograd (St. Petersburg), and sojourned in Germany and France before moving to the United States, see Marek Bartelik, *To Invent a Garden: The Life and Art of Adja Yunkers* (Easthampton, MA: Hudson Hills Press, 2000).

2. David Acton in exh. cat. *Adja Yunkers: Paintings, Drawings & Prints 1940-83* (New York: Associated American Artists, 1990), p. 12.

3. See, Leo Steinberg, 'Other Criteria,' first delivered as a lecture at the Museum of Modern Art, New York in 1968; reprinted in *Other Criteria: Confrontations with Twentieth-Century Art* (New York: Oxford University Press, 1972), pp. 55-91.

4. James Schuyler, review of *Adja Yunkers: Pastel Paintings and Drawings, 1956-1957* at Rose Fried Gallery, March 18 to April 6, 1957, *Artnews*, April 1957; reprinted in Schuyler, *Selected Art Writings* (New York: David R. Godine, 1998), p. 196.

5. Mark Rothko, 'Space in Painting' (ca. 1954) in *Writings on Art*, ed. Miguel López-Remiro (New Haven: Yale University Press, 2006), p. 112.

6. Indrikis Gelzis, email to the author, December 14, 2017.

7. Adja Yunkers, *Tiger's Eye* (New York), no. 8, June 1949; cited in Dore Ashton, *The New York School: A Cultural Reckoning* (Berkeley: University of California Press, 1992), pp. 188-89.

8. Paz, 'Objects and Apparitions' in *The Collected Poems*, p. 405.

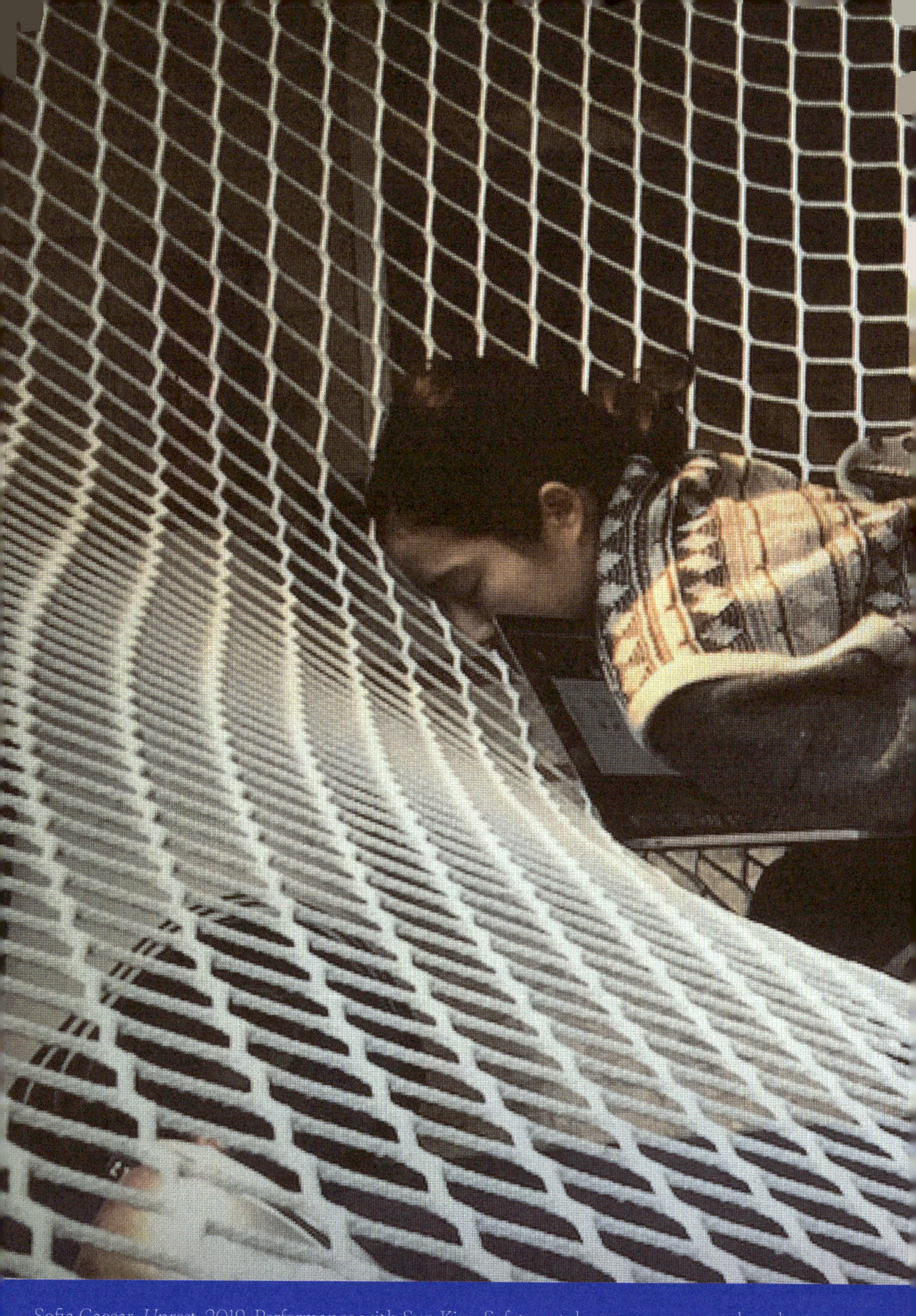

Sofia Caesar, *Unrest*, 2019, Performance with Sun Kim. Safety net, heaters, carpet, speakers, laptop, phones. Dimensions viable.

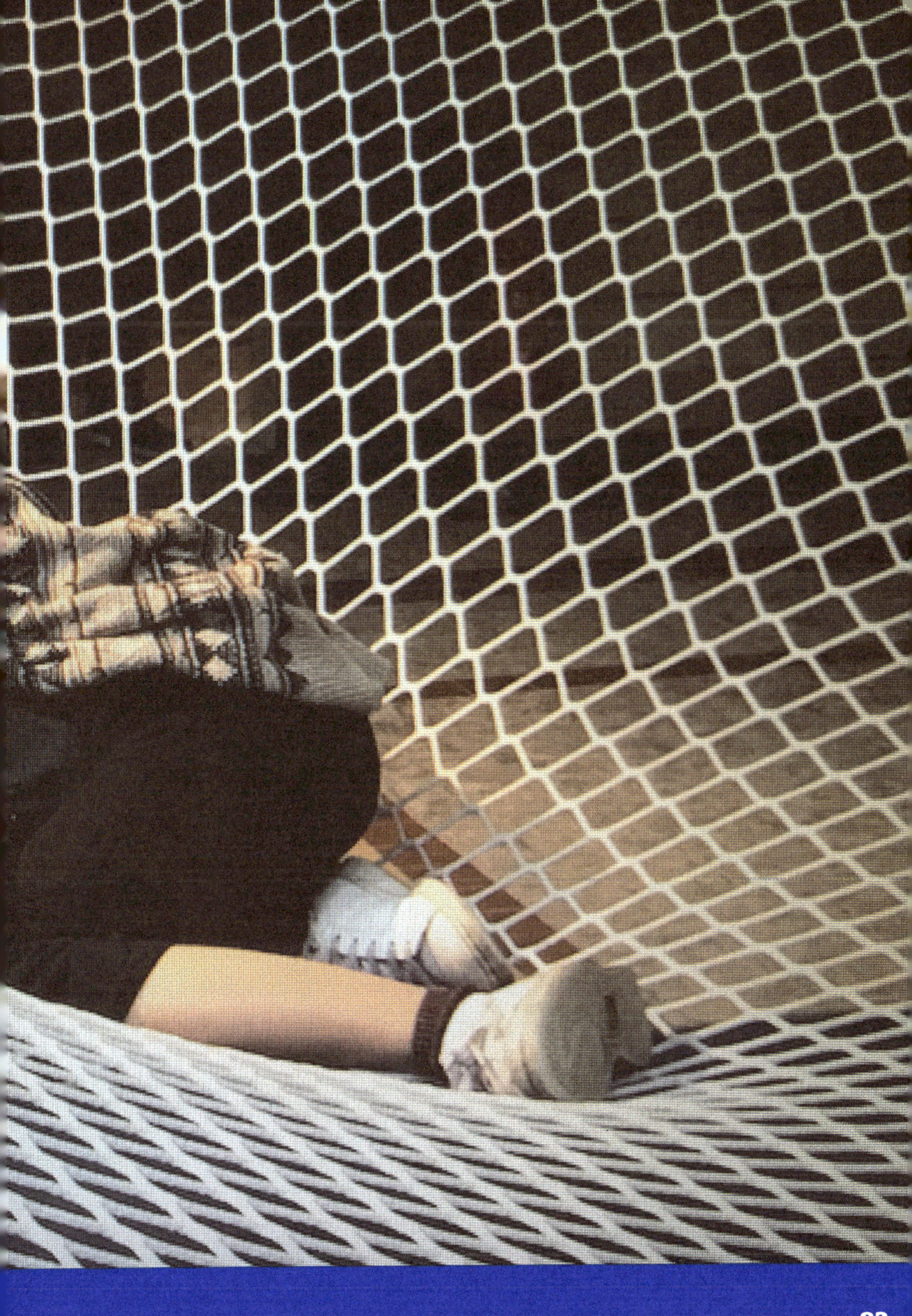

John C. Welchman (2025): This conversation was developed for inclusion in the catalogue for Island of Multiple Bridges, the 2019 HISK exhibition curated by Daniella Géo (November 21 to December 15, 2019) at Coupure Rechts 310, 9000 Ghent; it was published in an edited version available at: https://hisk.education/ volumes/publications/ An_island_of_multiple_bridges.pdf. The exhibition also featured work by Lisette de Greeuw, Francesca Ferreri, Eva Giolo, Johna Hansen, Megan-Leigh Heilig, Sina Hensel, Roel Heremans, Mirthe Klück, Hannah Mevis, Mark Požlep, Bárbara Sánchez Barroso, Gintautė Skvernytė, and Ingel Vaikla. Caesar recalls the immediate context of our discussion: 'It was winter, the building was cold and there was no heating.'

Caesar's work is formed around her experience of living with chronic illness, developing performance and video practices through dance and the exploration of somatic relationalities. We met in her HISK studio as the exhibition was being planned and prepared, surrounded by some of the objects and 'accessories' that it would feature. As parts of our discussion were still in the form of a raw transcription we edited and streamlined a bit; and I have added some notes on artists and exhibitions mentioned. After HISK Caesar studied for a PhD at LUCA School of Arts/KU Leuven, which was completed and conferred in 2024.

John C. Welchman (JCW): Before we get into it, let's think about the context. What are you planning for the HISK final show?

Sofia Caesar (SC): So, the first element I am working with is the heat, because the space has no heating. The exhibition will take place in an old veterinary school that was abandoned for years. Electricity, toilets, and all the infrastructure will be brought in by HISK just for the duration of the exhibition. HISK will provide me with three electric heaters, those kinds of outdoor spot heaters. I'm calling them 'fake suns' because most of them are called 'Sun'-something in the stores.

JCW: So, you want to put these throughout the space?

SC: Yes. They will be in a hall that has a sort of mezzanine with a gap in the middle. In this gap, I'm installing a safety net that is falling, which can be used as a hammock. But as people lie down in the net (*rede* in Portuguese means 'network,' 'hammock,' and 'net'–all at once), they slowly slide down due to the inclination. In this space there will also be heaters, a carpet, and some

Maintenance and Breakdown:

A Conversation between Sofia Caesar and John C. Welchman

pillows that I filled with cement. My idea is to do a performance in the space which will last twenty days.

JCW: That's the duration of the show?

SC: Yes. So, every day there will be a group of people that come to rest–and really insist on resting. I did this once before during the opening of the exhibition *Canseira* in Rio.[1] There, it wasn't so clear who was a performer and who was a member of the public; but at some point, someone would just fall asleep, and then it became clear. Or someone would slide from the net really slowly, and it again became clear. So, it's like this: pushing rest to another state that becomes a kind of dance.

JCW: The notion and experience of *ambience* are key to your work, I think. You seem to be interested in how ambience is a combination of things that are existing in a space, but accentuated by the inter-activity generated in a location as it is infiltrated by the prota-gonists who pass through it, right? In addition, there's always a sort of surplus, something that you can't account for in the space between the interactivity and the actual architecture or the design, and so on. This seems to be quite central to your thinking?

SC: I'm not sure what you mean by 'surplus.'

JCW: The surplus part is this thing you can't control. First of all, if you put into the space a combination of people who are normal visitors along with people who you had asked to be there, other 'visitors' wouldn't necessarily be able to distinguish between them. So, there would be a smudge or a blur between the two contexts. And then, secondly, you don't know what's going to happen. So, you don't know quite how the performers are going to 'perform' unless they have a really tight script, which I don't think they do.

SC: I don't think it will be tightly scripted, but there will be a routine. Like a daily routine where there's a time for each thing. But, yes, the work starts with these elements that intervene in the space: the falling net, heaters, carpet, and cement pillows, hopefully some heated pillows too. And then there are people, whether performers or visitors. The performers maintain the action of resting, which is, at the same time, work. It's the production of unproductiveness, bodies searching for different ways of relating to the objects in the space. And then phones and devices, which are a part of these people. From this inhabiting of the space, we will search for ways to break down the ambivalent actions of rest/work: fall, slide, rebel, refuse, splay, etc. But first we need heat.

JCW: The idea of *heating* interests me, because there's a moment in early Conceptual Art when the opposite of heating was used propositionally–by the British group Art & Language who wrote an article which, because of the way that they were investing in the definition of what might be 'conceptual,' was itself considered as a conceptual gesture: 'Remarks on Air-Conditioning: An Extravaganza of Blandness' (1967).[2] It ties into the question of ambience because, particularly in the United States, where there's a lot of air conditioning, a key articulation of the physical or material ambience of an interior space, as opposed to its social activation, would be kick-started by the air conditioning unit. The small noises it makes, the experience of air coming out, discernible effects of freshening and cooling. At stake here was an imagination that a work could be made about a recessional, behind-the-scenes material mechanism, something almost invisible, that quite literally produces an atmosphere. These ideas take us back to Impressionism, which was also predicated on atmospherics. The key words that Monet used so often in his correspondence were terms like 'atmosphere' and 'effect' (*effet*)–the latter standing for the spectrum of physicalized experiences that relate to the prevalence of foggy, sunny, rainy, or icy conditions.[3] Many of these situations obviously correlate with temperature, so it's interesting to see how we end up again with heating and cooling.

It seems to me, however, that using heat takes us in a slightly different direction, though a parallel one, in relation to these early investigations. You're dealing with the atmospheric envelope of a space, the very air that we breathe, and the way that that air feels is probably the baseline of the atmospherics of space. Maybe next you have the architecture, the painting of the walls, the physical envelope that encloses you. And then there are the things that are in the space beginning with architectural articulations like light fixtures or stairs or doors or windows, right? And then you have the supplemental objects in a space–its décor if you like. Put something on the wall and this begins to include art. So, it seems to me that you are intervening in the constitution and reception of all those elements.

SC: Yeah, the conditions.

JCW: So, you're going back to heating and going back to the difference between a visitor and a performer, which has been explored in the art world; but you're bringing into play the formative constituent elements of the production of the atmosphere of a space. Maybe it's here that your project 'begins'?

SC: Yes. The first title of *Canseira*, the exhibition in Brazil, was *Corpos que movem coisas que movem corpos* (Bodies That Move Things That Move Bodies). It came from the notion that we can move our own conditions with our gestures. That show was about moving the conditions of the ways in which we move, in particular the way leisure and work are entangled in the body, and how leisure is monetized.[4] So, when you talk about this constitution of things . . .

JCW: And the air conditioning. It's interesting how we use the word 'condition.' It's a funny word, *condition*, isn't it? The condition of something. Sometimes it simply means 'constitution.' But 'condition' is already informed by a cultural supplement: something is conditioned or in a condition. In the art world you have a 'condition report'–speaking to the way your work goes into a space, gets itemized and described; and then has to come out of the exhibition space in the same condition. Otherwise, there's a monetary penalty or an insurance claim or something. That's a very specific art world usage; but in other areas the word is often synonymous with the assisted production of an atmosphere.

SC: It's about 'support' as well, no? I didn't want to say this, but 'support structure.' I've been thinking about the word 'maintenance' a lot. Remembering Mierle Ladermanz Ukeles's *Manifesto for Maintenance Art* (1969).[5]

JCW: Well, 'maintenance' is another of those redolent words. For me it's also connected with Mike Kelley whose avatar was a projected fiction derived from a famous photo on the back of his survey exhibition catalogue *Catholic Tastes* (1993) of the artist dressed as a janitor. His father worked as a janitor in a school, and he sometimes took on that function himself, even as it was a projected persona it was also a bit of a fiction. So, you would have the janitorial blue overalls, and the mop and the bucket. And all the appurtenances of janitorial practice–in order, I think, both to refer to and disabuse his working-class origins.[6]

But maintenance and conditioning are surely two sides of the same thing. Maintenance is the manual aspect of the preservation and cleaning of a space. Conditioning is an aspect generally organized through automated functionality–like heating or cooling that happen at an infrastructural level. So, they're paired concepts, I think. Does your notion of maintenance relate to cleaning and janitorial things or were you going in a slightly different direction?

SC: It was the idea of maintaining the heat in the space, because it tends to go up. It tends to leave. It was not only about cleaning or keeping the space in order but thinking about this space where people come and maybe feel an attraction to it as a heated environment–as it's one of the few heated spaces in the building. The heat would also maintain the presence of people; it would condition the way that people inhabit the space. Invite relaxation. I am thinking about how this environment maintains itself.

JCW: Is maintenance about the continual adjudication of a status quo?

SC: What do you mean by 'adjudication'?

JCW: I mean the playing out, or the production of something–that also has an ordering impulse or a control mechanism behind it. Maybe 'status quo' isn't quite right, but there's something about a conservative threat.

SC: Yes, and the opposite would be breakdown!

JCW: If you're maintaining something, often what you're sustaining is habitability. You're maintaining the possibility that the space can continue to be occupied. Because it's cleaned, and it's painted or, you know, the architecture is not falling down, the windows are closing or opening, you put in double glazing . . . maintenance like that. In the rental economy in New York, they call the supplement that you have to pay when you rent an apartment the 'maintenance.' That's the fee for all the upkeep of the building that is shared, like the roof, the plumbing, electricity, water, heating, doorman, trash shoot, laundry room . . . all that stuff, the extra fee that you have to pay on a monthly basis. So, maintenance is counter-entropic, and it's capitalized. It's a capitalist term that's connected with the maintenance of value, amongst other things. That value can be translated from being a capital-directed supplement–where it primarily underpins financial, or real estate, value–into social terms. Maybe there could be a 'social

maintenance'? Perhaps you're speaking to the possibility that
the space can be occupied? In this case, what kind of activities
would transpire in the heated space?

SC: I have a list!

Slide down a safety net.
Use the wi-fi until you get tired.
Drain the battery of your phone.
Let your phone slide down to the ground.
Cuddle with your laptop.
Take a nap.
Caress your laptop.
Keep your friend warm.
Dream that you're dancing.
Charge your phone back up again. . .
and (I don't know if this is how you say this in English)
'lay under a fake sun.'
Play your favorite song.
Dance a little to kill the cold.
Drink too much coffee.
Gossip in the toilet.
Let the laziness hit you.
Insist on boredom.
Sit by the window.
Have an idea.
Move the heater around so it keeps a visitor warm.
Sit by the window again.
Let go of that weight in your limbs.
Fall slowly into a pile of pillows.
Feel that they are cold.
Try to start a fire.

'Try to start a fire' was the last one, because I realized it's
probably illegal.

JCW: Probably! But I suppose you could say 'light a match?'

SC: Yes.

JCW: It's funny, because most of these actions, activities, or
orientations, maybe more than half, are expressions of giving

in to entropy and dissipation. As energy drains out, as the body winds down, or goes to sleep, or retires. Or as things slip, or they fall, they are subject to the basic laws of energy, the basic laws of space, gravitation being chief among them, right? And then some of them are the opposite, maybe a quarter, are about recharging. So, they are counter-entropic. They rely on energy sources and power. Literally, you have to plug in the phone to the power source to charge it. In fact, in this case, HISK will have produced the electricity for the building, so this aspect ties in with the maintenance that HISK has to do on the whole building. Perhaps, in a sense, your intervention is a little meta-narrative of the whole situation of an art exhibition being programmed in a space that has been transitioned from pre-maintenance to maintenance. And you're acting in the space, in a way, that merges with what happens when a maintenance system has been put into place; but you're also contributing to that maintenance system because you've got the heat and you've occasioned other actions which are allegories of the situation that is being maintained.

SC: Entropy is definitely a force that recurs throughout my work. Centrifugal movements, slippages, noises. Usually there's a loop that is escaped from.

JCW: What's interesting, here, is that that then becomes a framing device for the things in your list. Because there's a kind of disjunction. Some activities aren't about entropy or its opposite, charging-up, like the invocation to dance a little, or dream of something. When you're evoking some kinds of human action the reaction has to be deeply personal . . . because one of the few things we can't do together is dream . . . or can we?

SC: Well, once I dreamed the same dream of a friend of mine whilst we were sleeping in the same bed. We had the same dream from different perspectives, each from our own personal perspectives, but we were in the same place, with the same people, doing the same things. It was strange.

JCW: I think that can happen but obviously it's quite rare. There's a project to look at about dream and community that the American British artist Susan Hiller did early in her career,

Dream Mapping (1974)–a topic to which she returned in 2000 when she curated *Dreammachine*, titled after an apparatus built by Brian Gysin and Ian Somerville in the late 1950s. So, dreaming at one level and dancing at another. Because dancing is a funny thing. You can certainly dance on your own, obviously, but then there's a sense that dance generally needs social or communal points of activation, right? So, the way to come out of this could be with a *part dance. . .* it's almost the escape valve for the piece.

SC: Yes, because in the performance we get so bored of lying down that at some point we need to move our bodies. The insistence on resting can be quite heavy. You get a bit high, or a bit drowsy, and at some point, you just have to move your body in a different way. Moments of running, jumping, or dancing, become implicitly urgent in the group at some point. We decide together without speaking about it: OK, now it's time to break out. Because we get bored of being bored.

JCW: What do you think this is about–making work that dwells so insistently on the opposite of unfurling? Maybe it's to do with *furling*: if you open out a flag you unfurl it; but to roll or fold it up is to furl it, if that word exists.

SC: Like rolling up a carpet?

JCW: Sort of, but that has a very different feel, doesn't it? Because the carpet is more utilitarian. Furling and unfurling betoken a sort of drama, and I suppose it's because of the symbolic. The reason we associate these actions with a flag is because it's a symbolic declaration. Once the thing is revealed it's redolent with national identity, or group solidarity, and so it's a very potent symbol. But I'm interested in what's at stake in thinking about that switch-off and *furl*, about submitting to gravity, closing or winding down, that kind of thing. To me the bottom -line referent is death. One step further . . . and the body doesn't wind down, it switches off. So, it's always one step on the other side of the ultimate entropic moment, which is where we all go back to in the end. The soil. That's a pretty heavy reference and maybe one of the reasons that you're doing this is to stage the rehabilitation of the body and the snatching away of death. It's a force of rejuvenation or revivification. And dance might be one way, a dream might be another; and there might be other ways still.

SC: It's funny, there has been a lot of stillness in the works I've made. But there's also jumping. And a loop that keeps on coming back, being pulled outward by tangents toward another thing. I'd note that unfurling is a movement that reminds me of the colonial gesture, as in the unfurling of the flag that is planted on top of a mountain as an act of domination. So, if furling is the undoing of a symbolic gesture, maybe it's the undoing of that process of consumption.

A countermovement. Some kind death needs to happen so another form of life can begin. And so, we can find other ways of moving. It's more an attempt to kill the dynamics that entrap the body, to, yes, rejuvenate or resuscitate it, but as a different body. Because if my rest is productive, if I'm working while I'm in the hammock, better reset this machine, no? Better caress that phone, or let it fall to the floor, instead of letting it have you. This reminds me of something I wrote last week: maybe these things I make are just things in the end. But they are things with souls, intelligent things—just as all things are intelligent—but we forget they are, so we can consume them. Or maybe the things I make come from a personal wish: to undo the me. A whispered wish: take my body and show me all the things that make it move the way it does, and then undo the me.

JCW: Jumping is interesting because it is the most dramatic, defiant, and futile effort to break through gravity. Humans can only jump just a little bit. We're not like fleas—which can apparently jump two hundred times their body length, something phenomenal. I mean for us this is ridiculous. Unless we're trained high jumpers, we can jump a couple of feet in the air, if we're lucky; it's the most insistent demonstration that we are bound by gravity. You have to expend a huge amount of energy to get a couple of feet up in the air. And then you come down instantly. There's one moment in philosophy that's structured around the sort of morbid inevitability of the gravitational pull, and it comes from Schopenhauer, the German philosopher. One of his fundamental principles turned on the notion that life itself, evanescence, vitality, and growth, was, effectively, a counter-gravitational exertion. He wrote about plants—which sprout, burgeon, bloom, and blossom. They grow up and produce canopies and spreads. He was struck by one exception, as he saw it, in the vegetal world: the tree that grows so that its branches flow downward, the 'weeping willow.' It's all there in the colloquial name: the tree that cries, the tree that mourns its own burgeoning. This observation produced a very interesting moment in his philosophy, as Schopenhauer tied the implications of this arboreal despondency into the very design of the countergravitational thrust that defines life itself.

So, what else will be in the space? There are a lot of actions and many inactions. Some might be there already, some you might program, others arise?

SC: I feel like the piece comes to rest in the repetition of the everyday routine of resting in the space, in the repetition of actions that tend to happen every day, like the coffee breaks, naps, and so on. The most important thing is to try to seek moments of breaking-out, of undoing idle actions. I'm interested in moments when for a second, we escape the dynamics that capture rest—moments suffused by noise, complexity, ambivalence. That is how this whole thing started, in a way. One day I was laying down in the hammock on my phone, and I was Googling a word that I had just heard about from Julie Van Elslande of Caveat, the word 'workation.'[7] On the results page I found an image of a man in a hammock, working. But I was in a hammock working. I had my computer on my lap; I had a smartphone in my hand. The guy had a computer on his lap, a smartphone in his hand. So, I asked myself, how can I break out of this? I tried to let the weight of my head go, and the fabric of the hammock under my head slipped away. So, I let my head fall, and it took with it the rest of my body. I fell on the ground. That's how the work with the yellow carpet started (*Workation*, 2019).[8] And I think this breaking-out moment, this gesture that allows the dynamics to be pulled to another direction, that's the thing that I need to seek.

JCW: Sure. Maybe this is about what work is against, what work is not. Leisure and downtime. Work becomes the forced production of the counter-gravitational push. Of life, to relax. It's another name for the space of what you are obliged or forced to do, in the name of economic necessity, or whatever it might be. Perhaps this ties in the punctuation marks within the field of lassitude . . . I think that's your word. Is it the translation of the title of your show?!

SC: Sounds very beautiful. Lassitude. Yes!

JCW: Finally, we got there. I knew we would get there!

SC: Yeah. But I think *canseira* is a bit less than that. I think lassitude is more lethargic.

JCW: 'Lethargic' will be a little more extreme, maybe. Because being lethargic is sloth-like. It's only one manner of general inactivity. It's really being switched off. Whereas 'lassitude' is a bit more elastic as I think your word is. But maybe *canseira* sits in the middle between lethargy and lassitude.

SC: Sluggishness?

JCW: Yes, but perhaps 'sluggishness' is more like lethargy. I like 'lassitude' because it's a touch more formal. LAS-SIT-UDE. It sounds out a grander turndown.

SC: Because the situation there will start from this ambivalence. People who are there are resting and they're at work at the same time. That's a bit like our trap nowadays. Rest is being made productive, it's monetized. How do we get out of this?

JCW: You mean the paradox that arises as people are commissioned to act the part of not working?

SC: That can be a trap.

JCW: I feel that's come up before in Tino Sehgal's work, this idea of trying to commission people to do nothing–or something that's consumed by the ritual of doing. It's a kind of art world luxury, isn't it?

SC: Yes. It's quite something. There's a sentence about all this I find to be brilliant. It's in the text that Raphael Fonseca wrote for my exhibition *Canseira* in Brazil. It's something like: 'The rest of some is the punishment of others.'[9] It's difficult to explain because 'punishment' or 'travail' is in the root of the Portuguese word for work, *trabalho*. There's definitely something here. The use of play in the world of work today; the constant self-performance in social media; the instrumental side of participatory art–who gets to work while being in a hammock, or in a warm bed? Where and how can we situate the maintenance of people's rest? What's on the unseen side of this coin? How are colonial structures woven into and through these questions?

JCW: Another term that connects with all this–especially with the object of maintenance–is *equilibrium*. I mean, maintenance wants to produce the best possible equilibrium for a space. There's an efficiency quotient here too: efficient maintenance tends to equilibrium.

SC: Like an ecosystem.

JCW: But ecosystems are much more subject to entropic conditions.

SC: Yeah, they tend to do chaos. I just remembered *Condensation Cube* when you said that.

JCW: The Hans Haacke piece?

SC: Yes. I also thought of the aquariums of Pierre Huyghe.[10]

JCW: Huyghe's work is interesting because he's creating a dysfunctional conjugation of different plants and animals, almost an atopia. He brings them together as interference zones. So, you have things that ants do, what insects do, or crustaceans; and you have mammalian interventions that just operate on a different level. And then they would all be configured around human programming and presence. I think that's what's interesting in his work: he layers these operating strata almost archaeologically.

SC: This notion of 'atopia' is interesting to me. It hit me in relation to my approximation work with the images of the Hélio Oiticica installations next to the Google offices.[11] Because Oiticica used this word *crelazer*, which means something like *creleisure*. It's a mix of leisure, creation, and belief–in one word. It's about the belief in leisure as a creative force, or leisure as the creation of belief, but there's always a play between the three words. We situate Oiticica historically as kind of utopian artist; his radical gestures produced different ways of inhabiting spaces, and different bodies. A lot of people ask me if my work is dystopian. Or if it explores a kind of self-aware utopia.

JCW: But there's something about your work that always has to do with *congregationality*. It's to do with the conjunction of congregations, how people occupy a space at leisure or at work, or in another condition of dreaming, or whatever it might be. It's very much staged around the premise of social interaction. And that could be a mode of social interaction that relates to work, art, or leisure.

But actually, I think that your work is at the interface between those three places. You're interested in the place where all of these 'conditions' are also possibilities that bleed into each other.

1. *Canseira*, one-person exhibition by Sofia Caesar, curated by Raphael Fonseca, Centro de Arte Hélio Oiticica, Rio de Janeiro, Brazil (September 5 to November 30, 2019).

2. Art & Language (Michael Baldwin, b. 1945), 'Remarks on Air-Conditioning: An Extravaganza of Blandness,' *Arts Magazine* (November 1967), pp. 22-23.

3. For an account of the significance of temporal indicators in Impressionism, see John C. Welchman, 'Monet and the Development of a Nominative Effectualism,' chapter 2 of *Invisible Colors: A Visual History of Titles* (New Haven and London: Yale University Press, 1997), pp. 49-80.

4. Cesar notes that she 'also thought about calling the exhibition: *Rooms to Keep out the Words That Choreograph Us.*'

5. Beginning in 1977, Mierle Laderman Ukeles worked for decades as an official, unsalaried artist-in-residence at New York's Department of Sanitation. She wrote 'MANIFESTO FOR MAINTENANCE ART, 1969! – Proposal for an exhibition: "CARE" in 1969'; see https://feld-mangallery.com/exhibition/manifesto-for-maintenance-art-1969.

6. Mike Kelley used the symbolism and attire–and for the photograph on the back cover of *Catholic Tastes*, ed. Elizabeth Sussman (New York: Whitney Museum of American Art and Harry M. Abrams, 1993), adopted the persona–of a janitor. He referred to dirt and cleaning in *Seventy-Four Garbage Drawings and One Bush* (1988), *Deodorized Central Mass with Satellites* (1991-99) and other works.

7. Julie Van Elslande is a founding member of Caveat (caveat.be), together with Florence Cheval and Rony Heiremans. Caveat was an organization that addressed art and contemporary labor practices. Van Elslande collaborated with Caesar on the workshop *Workation* at SB34 in Brussels in 2020.

8. *Workation: O dia em que aprendi a dizer (The Day I Learned to Say)* (2019) is an installation with four looped videos, yellow carpet, a big screen, a small screen, laptop, smartphone, and cushions which created a landscape in-between office and beach that invites passers-by to experience ambivalent relaxation. As people enter the work, they might take out their phones and find themselves repeating gestures present in the videos. See: https://vimeo.com/353834797?-fl=pl&fe=vl.

9. Raphael Fonseca is a curator and critic, currently curator of modern and contemporary Latin American art at the Denver Art Museum. His work includes a lecture-form meditation on his archive of more than nine hundred images of hammocks, 'To and Fro: Inventions of Brazil in the Swing of a Hammock' (June 5, 2018), in which he discussed tropes of 'laziness' and sloth associated with 'Brazilianness.' Fonseca curated and provided an exhibition text for *Canseira*.

10. Pierre Huyghe has created several works using aquariums, including *Zoodram 6* (2013); *Cambrian Explosion 19* (2013); *Abyssal Plane* (2015); and *Circadian Dilemma (El Día del Ojo)* (2017)–exhibited together in *Pierre Huyghe: liminal*, Punta della Dogana, Venice (March 17 to November 24, 2024).

11. *Aproximações (Cosmococas / Escritorios)* (Approximations [Cosmococa / Office]) (2019) took the form of computer screenshots enlarged on the wall. To the left are installation shots of the Cosmococa series by Neville D'Almeida and Helio Oiticica. On the right, images of a corporate office (such as Google).

One of the key operating parameters for *(Le Plus Objet des Objets)* is stealth. While the event was announced in a formal invitation in January 2020 as the last in a cycle of four associated performances some weeks after the opening in October 2019 of an exhibition at the Zadkine Museum in Paris (*L'Instinct de la matière*), no further information about it was posted. There was no associated wall text or handout; and during the ensuing event the artist herself did not directly enter the space. Visitors could see no stage or performers—nothing that pointed to anything answering to the event; no visible trace, in fact, of something that to all appearances seemed not to be taking place. Visitors were only alerted to the possibility that they had been unwitting participants in, or witnesses to, the event when they left the space and were given a numbered and stamped slip of paper attesting to their presence and imbrication in whatever it was that had transpired. This *Accusé de Participation* functions, simultaneously, as a receipt and attestation, but also—as both the French original and its English translation suggest—as a means of accusation.

But there was more than stealth at stake here. The action was subject to plausible deniability, as the officers of the museum and the exhibition's curator, brushed off or deflected any inquiries about the event and seemed—or claimed—to have no knowledge about

En Garde: Katya Ev

it. Stealth, redundancy and deniability thus combined to frame the event as a kind of fraud or deception; or, at the very least, a secret of some kind ordained by a non-disclosure agreement that was itself undisclosed.

2.
Katya Ev's setup replaced and augmented all of the invigilating and supervisory staff who would normally work at the reception desk, the security station outside the galleries, and, as attendants, in the exhibition galleries themselves. Normally numbering around half a dozen, for her opening night event, Ev commissioned eleven performers, camouflaging them in plain sight in the same kind of casual-smart attire that their opposite numbers in real life might have worn; and effectively replicating their 'standard' age and apparent gender profiles. From within these disguises, however, the surrogate protago-nists represented a cross-section of individuals chosen because of their capacities to simulate, order, or even control by way of the rhetoric of exchange associated with a public situation: some were theatrically trained actors or performance-seasoned musicians; and the group included the head bouncer from an underground techno-music club and a dominatrix.

The artist's careful selection of 'actors' offered partially to pre-empt the concept of a performance directive. She relied on a number of key capacities, orchestrated by a combination of personality and profession, including the ability to instruct or command in ways that were not ostentatious or conspicuous; an awareness of the formality, ritual, and politesse of the museum space, so that the actors could inhabit the protocol of a guard, using a plausible repertoire of ges-tures and phrases associated with the function. But effective simula-tion of museological normality was at the same time over-coded by action mandates that subtly flouted or exceeded this basic framework of reference by making recourse to a manner that, as the artist puts it, 'would be delicately subversive, or absurd, or inadequate.' By way of instructions that might be mildly contradictory, or repetitive, or accompanied by gestural or linguistic accents that somehow exceeded– but only in small increments–the visitor's threshold of expectation or awareness, Ev sought to precipitate and unravel the coercive constitu-tion of art-denominated institutional space.

The 'training' of the performers was a kind of interactive seminar predicated on 'rules of engagement' that emphasized a number of strategies giving rise to a general mode of situation-correlated exaggeration. The impersonating guards would respond both proactively

and reactively to the social horizons of the behavior
that unfolded around them, interposing facetious even
ridiculous routines of advice and prohibition sanctioned by and drawing on their unquestioned authority.
A visitor standing some distance from an artwork might
be enjoined to 'please move closer . . . a bit more,
please.' When performed seamlessly, this patent reversal
of the usual injunction in museums to 'stand back' and
'keep your distance' might itself appear completely
normal; and reluctant viewers would–unselfconsciously–
find themselves in compliance. Ev marshalled an array
of these control conditions: the nature and direction
of viewer itineraries; behavior modifications; and a
spate of cautions and warnings. Each was enacted and
delivered by drawing on the resources of authority and
conviction vested in the vocational arbitration of professional invigilation and secured by unquestioning
public sanction.

3.
(Le Plus Objet des Objets) thus addresses the opacity,
arbitrariness, and secrecy of the rule-governed orchestration of museum or gallery space. It foregrounds the
overriding mechanism of control by which these zones
are ordered and disciplined: that of surveillance. To
this end, it magnifies and italicizes the consequences
of the coercive regimen by giving rise to countermand-
ing episodes fraught with humor, parody, contradiction,
and even intimations of punishment. Above all, the
project reveals the contours of the manufacture of
consent by way of conformist obedience–a declaration
more remarkable because most of the museum-going public would never imagine that their volition could be
short-circuited or deferred.

At the same time, the title, *(Le Plus Objet des Objets)*, borrowed from Gilles Deleuze, points to the nesting of objects within hierarchies or groups; and, beyond this, to the defining relationality between subject and object. By foregrounding the structures that underwrite and manage social objectification within the museum as a system of objects, Ev points to a fundamental trans-mutation between orders of identification as objects are consumed by tactical subjectivities; subjects are objectified by routines of surveillance; and the event itself inhabits its invisibility by way of transgressions transacted through covert masquerade.

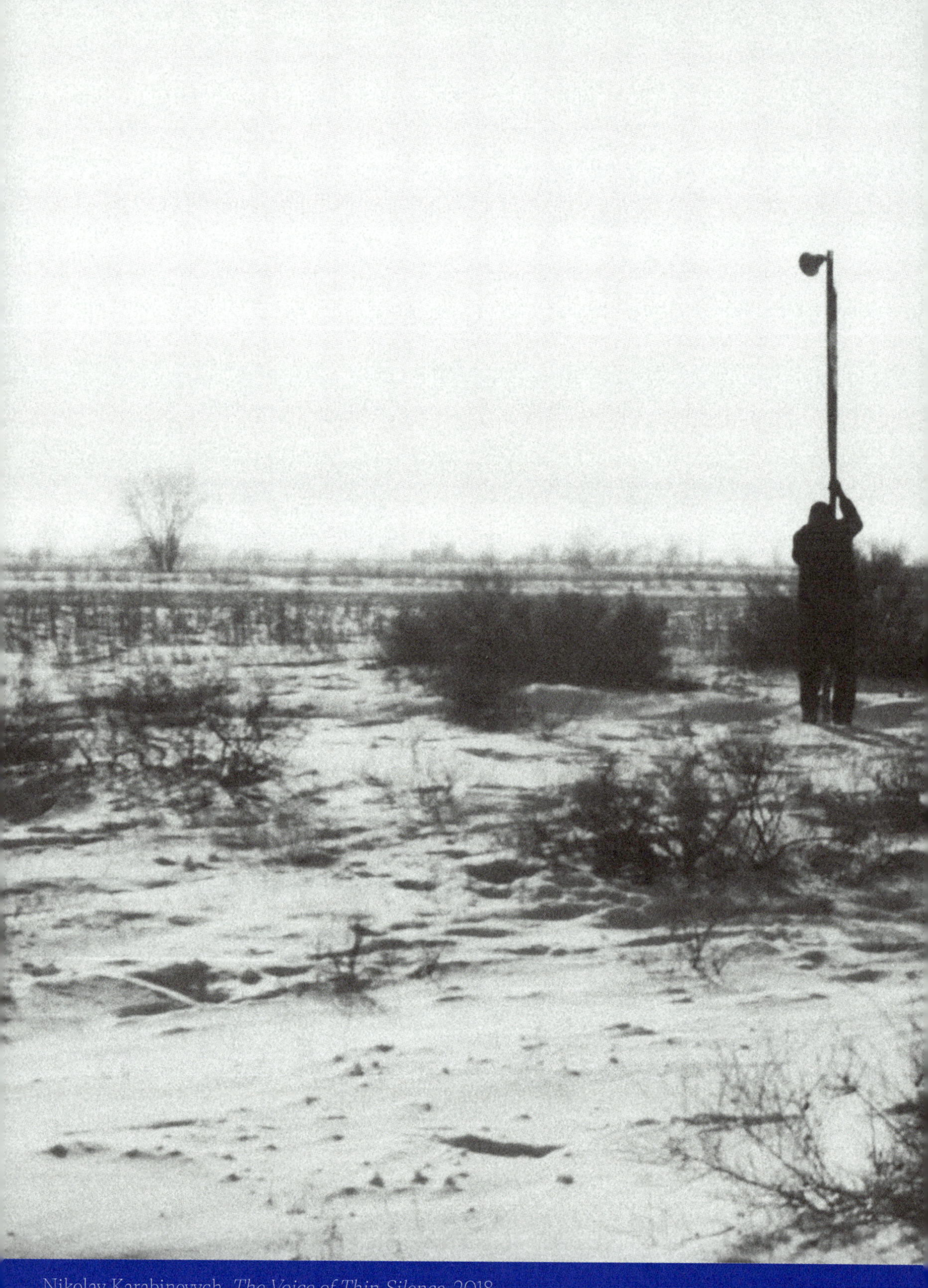

Nikolay Karabinovych, *The Voice of Thin Silence*, 2018.
Analog black-and-white photograph on Baryta paper. (©)

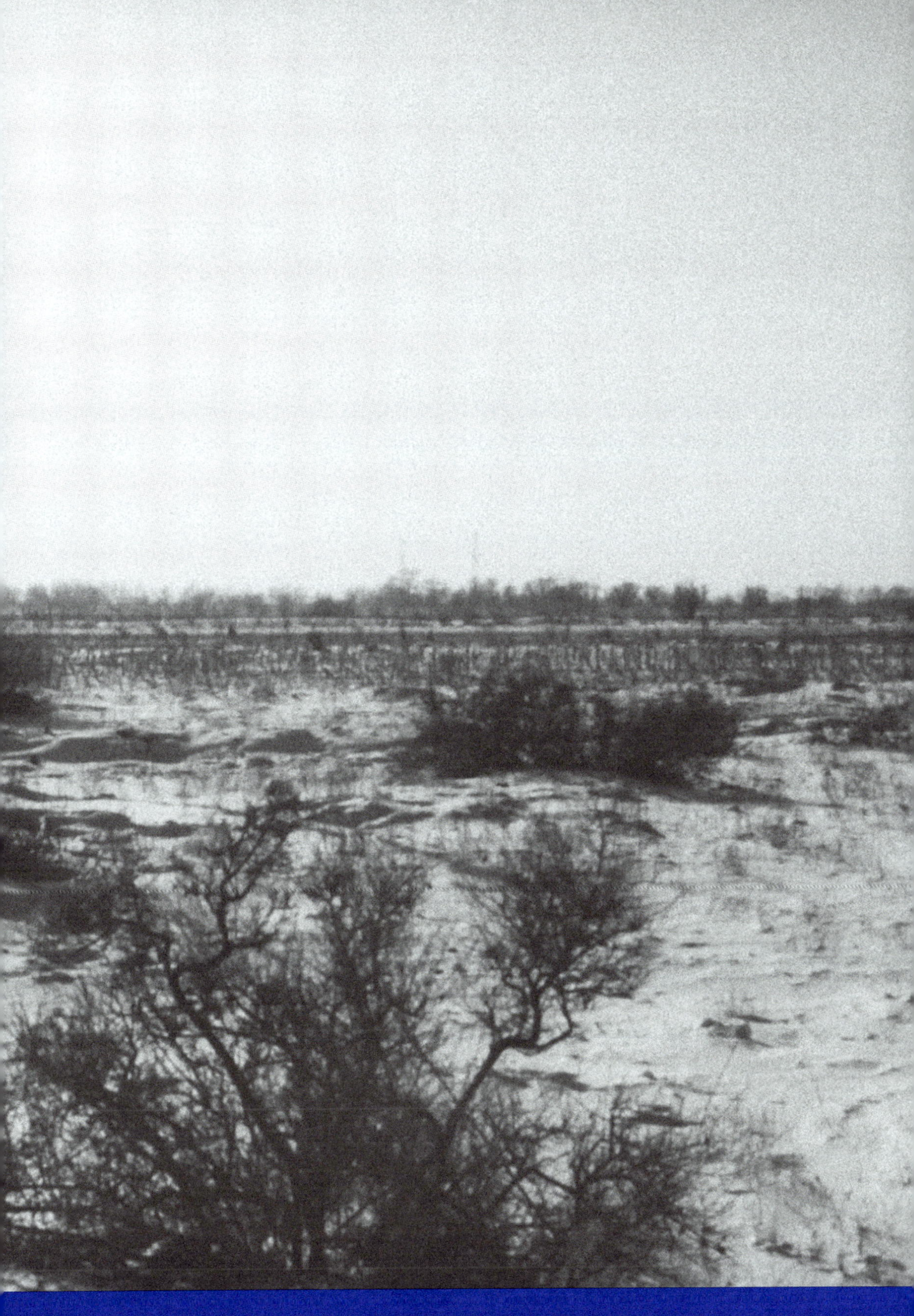

John C. Welchman (2025): This essay and the work it addresses were completed after the annexation of Crimea in 2014 but before Russia's military invasion of Ukraine and the ensuing war that began in February 2022 and is, tragically, still being waged. I have a special interest in Ukraine as I spent four consecutive winters in the former Soviet Union from 1989-92 during the collapse and dissolution of the USSR, including sojourns in Abkhazia, Crimea (where I spent New Year's Eve 1992 with Mustafa Dzhemilev in a cave complex in Bakhchysarai shortly after he became 1st Chairman of the Mejlis of the Crimean Tatar People the previous year), Odesa, Kyiv, the eastern Carpathian mountains, and rural Moldova. Karabinovych's research into the Pontic Greeks resonated deeply with stories of exile, loss (and sometimes return) that I heard from Tatars, Germans, and other minorities in Ukraine, southern Russia, and the Caucasus.

In discussion (summer 2025) Karabinovych notes that 'the title Ukrainians: The People Who Couldn't Go Home was initially read—in 2018—as a layered reflection on diaspora and underground cultural networks. But after February 24, 2022 it has taken on a tragically literal meaning: millions of Ukrainians quite literally cannot return home due to destruction and war. My work has also explored diaspora as a long-term cultural survival model, focusing on the Ukrainian émigré community in Manchester, active since 1949. In hindsight, it anticipates aspects of how Ukrainian culture may now continue, and survive, through new waves of migration and displacement across the world.'

The essay was first published in the HISK end-of-year exhibition In a Long Blink of an Eye curated by Daniella Géo in the Gosset building on Rue Gabrielle Petit, Brussels (December 17, 2020 to January 31, 2021).

Zapovit (Testament): Nikolay Karabinovych

1. À la recherche

The motor force of the work of Nikolay Karabinovych turns on the fulcrum of historical research, or, more precisely, on a series of inquiries into the production and reception of histories–so that what they pivot around is also part of a shifting system of meaning and value. The histories in question are set among a wide array of personal, genealogical, geographical, and cultural horizons that converge on what the artist has termed the construction and circulation of 'fluid identities' in Eastern Europe after the demise of its socialist regimes beginning in the mid-1980s. In some works, such as *The Voice of Thin Silence* (2018), the quotients of history and autobiography furnish points of departure and gestures of materialization that are directly orchestrated by the historical record.

In this case, Karabinovych and his father made a journey to the village of Shelek (or Chilik) in Kazakhstan, where his great-grandfather had been exiled with those identified as ethnic Greeks–along with other displaced minorities, including Chechens and Volga Germans–after World War II. Predicated on Joseph Stalin's abundant and accelerating paranoia, the deportations were a mode of state-decreed ethnic cleansing that started in the 1930s with the forced relocation of some three million *kulaks*, peasants, and minorities and continued apace during and after the war, when another three and a half million ethnic minorities were forcibly uprooted and moved to mostly remote locations in Siberia and Central Asia before Stalin died in 1953. Attrition rates were appalling, with as many as 43 percent of exiles dying en route or on arrival, of disease or starvation in their unfamiliar and often inhospitable new environments.

Ranged along the Black Sea coast and hinterland of present-day Ukraine, Crimea, and the Caucasus, the Pontic Greeks, like the Crimean Tatars and other non-Slavic minorities (Kalmyks, Chechens, Ingush, Balkars, Karachays, Meskhetian Turks, and even a small population of Crimean Italians), were condemned en masse as sympathizers of the Axis powers and systematically purged from a region where they had lived for centuries–and, in the case of the Greeks, for some two millennia. One of the largest deportations occurred from May to June 1944, when some 200,000 Crimean Tatars along with 37,000 Armenians, Bulgarians, and Greeks–the latter numbering around 15,000–were dispatched to Uzbekistan and Kazakhstan (that Karabinovych's great-grandfather was deported half a decade later, in 1949, testifies to the repetition and inexorability of the waves of cleansing).[1]

The Soviet displacements were part of larger currents of reflex xenophobia that defined the first half of the twentieth century, from the pogroms in Eastern-Europe between the 1880s and early 1900s and the Armenian genocide (1915-16) through to the ultimate atrocity of the Holocaust; but which included waves of pogroms in the later nineteenth and early twentieth centuries, the 'repatriations' of Soviet citizens sanctioned by the Allied Powers after World War II, and the wartime internment of Japanese Americans, and the McCarthy 'trials' of the early 1950s in the United States.

Two generations removed from the events of the 1940s, having lived with almost none of their direct consequences, Karabinovych resolved to face and reflect on how to mark or otherwise intervene in the history and experience of his great-grandfather's exile. What could be flagged or put into question in this regard? And on what terms and with what possible consequences and effects?

If *The Voice of Thin Silence* engages—at least at first—with history as a dark, foreboding, and fateful sentence of exile, Karabinovych's other work has unfolded in a series of collisions with different—and parallel—effects of historical reckoning. *In Ukrainians: The People Who Couldn't Go Home* (2018), for example, the artist makes recourse to a *transhistorical* negotiation between a popular cultural event and a construct of identity funded by a pair of moments—both animated by what we could term export culture—that were brought together by chance in (the recording of) a 1981 concert by the Manchester new wave band New Order (formed by vocalist and guitarist Bernard Sumner, bassist Peter Hook, and drummer Stephen Morris in 1980, and joined by Gillian Gilbert on keyboards later that year) at the Ukrainian National Home, a speakeasy on Second Avenue in Manhattan's Lower East Side. Around the year that the artist's great-grandfather was deported to Kazakhstan—roughly the same distance east of Manchester that New York is to the West—the émigré community of Little Ukraine reached a peak population of some 60,000.

Prompted by a seemingly random outcropping of fortuitous symmetry, the premise of *Ukrainians: The People Who Couldn't Go Home* is built on a gesture of transhistorical overlay already present in the artist's found material. For the VHS tape of New Order's East Village gig, shot and edited by Michael Shamberg, is launched by establishing shots of a portrait of the Ukrainian national poet Taras Schevchenko hanging above the venue's stage, after which the recording was titled.[2] This gesture of situational improvisation cross-hatches a live performance of emblematically laconic Mancunian post-punk sound with the figure of the Ukrainian laureate—also an ethnographer, painter, and illustrator—who was born a serf in 1814, revivified the 'Little-Russian' language (as Ukrainian was pejoratively described in the nineteenth century), and was, like Karabinovych's great-grandfather a century later, involuntarily dispatched to Kazakhstan.[3]

2. Axis ('it's amazing how rubbery you can be when you're not expecting something')[4]

Ukrainians: The People Who Couldn't Go Home amplifies the dissonant conjugation of these events by subjecting them to further rounds of apparently decontextualized insinuation. The structure of the work eventuates by way of an axial rotation or selective augmentation of the historical record that crystalizes another order of relationality–governed by neither fate nor decree, on the one hand, nor by the jumps and lacunae of transhistorical juxtaposition, on the other. Instead, Karabinovych twists and supplements the coincident events that funded his points of departure by means of various principles of recasting and restaging. The axis does double service here, standing for both the route between these contingencies and the (sometimes rubbery) turns they necessitate and provoke.

For *Ukrainians: The People Who Couldn't Go Home*, the artist commissioned a cover version of New Order's *Chosen Time* rendered by eleven members of the Manchester-based Orlyk folk dance ensemble along with two accordionists. The idea of 'covering' supplies much of the rotational energy of this work: in addition to another group standing in for the 'original'–but utilizing different musical and dance idioms–Karabinovych re-mobilizes the first track on the VHS tape (which broke out after the Schevchenko zoom) and thus uncovers and reaffirms the founding cultural elision between transatlantic post-punk and Ukraine. Further, the grounds of the covering are rooted in a construct of time pointed to in the title of the New Order track. Founded only a year before their East Village gig, following the suicide in 1980 of Joy Division principal Ian Curtis, the lyrics of New Order's first LP, *Movement*, were haunted by this loss and the questions it provoked. *Chosen Time* seems to allude to these circumstances by negotiating ambiguously between the temporal frameworks of choice and destiny—which correlate, more or less, with the coordinates we have already marked: the free calibrations of the transhistorical, and the tragic eventuations of fate. The covering at stake in *Ukrainians: The People Who Couldn't Go Home* thus posits the overlay of these two reckonings with time but refuses the polarization between them by opening up other rounds of reference.

In another reprise of the situational logic underwriting the Ukrainian National Home concert and tape, Karabinovych appropriated his title from a 1978 BBC documentary, *Ukrainians: The People Who Couldn't Go Home*, a borrowing that simultaneously underscores the association of Ukrainian national identity with emigration and migration and folds in a humorous allusion to the nocturnal nomadism of the post-punk and associated club scenes in the United States and United Kingdom in the early 1980s. In addition, a number of satellite pieces comment, sometimes mischievously, on the framing devices of the project itself. Notable is an arrangement that interposes a copy of the New Order VHS tape between volumes three and four of a five-book set of the writings of Shevchenko, thus transforming the books into bookends and the tape (now an axis passing through) into a bookmark set in their midst.

Karabinovych brought fate into contact with contingency by mobilizing another musical commission—this time from the Berlin-based musician, DJ, and producer Yuriy Gurzhy.[5] The artist asked for a work in dialogue with the plaintive, rhythmically innovative *rebetiko* an early- and mid-twentieth-century fusion of Greek and Anatolian musical traditions. Rebetiko emerged as part of the gangster and drug den underworlds of Smyrna, Athens, and Piraeus; it was associated early on with urban poverty, protest, and disenfranchisement, and deeply marked by the genocide of Pontic and Anatolian Greeks in the 1920s and 1930s, often referred to as the Asia Minor Catastrophe.[6] Collaborating with some of the Greek inhabitants of Chilik, Karabinovych set up a makeshift pole in the outskirts of town, topped by a loudspeaker wired to broadcast Gurzhy's tribute composition into the enveloping steppe beyond the city limits.

Bracketed by almost futile sonic dissemination from a lone high speaker seemingly abstracted from a concentration camp perimeter, the artist offered the project a poetic-cum-theological subtext by way of a title borrowed from the first Book of Kings in the Old Testament. There, the prophet Elijah is party to a divine exchange on Mount Sinai in the form of what is referred to as a 'gentle breeze,' or 'the still, thin voice of silence.' As the Russian critic Viktor Misiano notes, the communicative diminuendo (gentle, still, thin . . . silent) pointed to in the biblical text is prefaced by a series of violent eruptions of natural forces (wind, earthquake, and fire) which order the experience of prophetic inspiration by way of a paradoxical couplet: as earth-rending power is combined with the beatitude of an unfathomable immediacy engendered by (almost) soundless communion.[7]

As my own grandfather, W. E. Booth Taylor, noted in his study, *The Prophetic Word*, completed in 1945, a few years before Karabinovych's great-grandfather was sent into exile, however one understands the rule of God over history and the larger 'Providence that overrules,' these superscriptions must always be set against 'the deadly peril of [the] national and religious exclusivism' that ravaged Europe in the mid-twentieth century.[8] Yet, the matter is not so simple. First, Yahweh's divine ordination is not manifest in the dramatic or sublime reorderings of nature with which Elijah is at first confronted–and in which the scripture insists God was not present (though He may have delivered)–but is, instead, camouflaged in that almost imperceptible 'still . . . voice' (sometimes translated as 'a delicate, whispering voice'). This voice, secondly, delivers a number of mandates to the prophet about royal and religious succession; proscriptions, followed by Elijah, that give rise to a purge from Syria and Israel of all who do not conform to the monotheistic diktat predicated on renouncing the worship of Baal. The two anointed kings and Elijah's successor thus act as territorial and providential guarantors of the cleansing from the region of all worship not in conformity with Jewish monotheism.

While Karabinovych's Chilik project refers most immediately to the disaggregation of futility associated with a sound that peters out into the adjacent vastness—a message that is lost, physically, in its own faint resonance, but endures in the form of manifest destiny—there is a more powerful message caught up in the paradox of prophecy itself. For any attempt to legislate the future, especially one fortified by divine imperative, is founded on the subjugation of those who are deemed to stand outside the purview of what will be delivered. In this light, any mode of prophesy uttered on behalf of a religious, ethnic, or national formation is itself complicit with the cleansing—or annihilation—of whatever or whoever stands in its way. This uncomfortable paradox is one of the several means by which Karabinovych comes to terms with the contingent imprint of history and the contradictions everywhere apparent in the drive not just to improve or perfect it, but also to remember . . . and to revise.

[1] Karina V. Korostelina, *Social Identity and Conflict: Structures, Dynamics, and Implications* (New York: Springer, 2007), p. 9.

[2] In 2001 the tape was remastered and rereleased on DVD as *New Order 3 16* by Warner Music Vision and London Records, combining the nine tracks of the November 18, 1981 concert at the Ukrainian National Home (Taras Shevchenko) with the eleven tracks of New Order's performance at the Reading Festival, August 30, 1998.

[3] While in exile in the Russian military garrison in Orenburg, near the Ural Mountains, Shevchenko was seconded on the *Konstantin* as part of the first Russian naval expedition to the Aral Sea in 1848.

[4] Peter Hook, last sentence of the entry '19 November 1981: New Order play the Ukrainian National Home, New York,' in *Substance: Inside New Order* (London: Simon & Schuster, 2014), p. 82.

[5] Founder of the band Emigrantski Raggamuffin Kollektiv RotFront (a world music fusion of reggae, ska, dancehall, klezmer, and hip hop) in 2003, Yuriy Gurzhy compiled *Borsh Division: Future Sound of Ukraine*, released by Trikont in 2016.

[6] See Jim Sclavunos (drummer of Nick Cave's The Bad Seeds), 'So Good, They Made It Illegal," *The Guardian*, Sunday April 18, 2004 [available at https://www.theguardian.com/culture/2004/apr/19/guesteditors3]; and Gail Holst-Warhaft, *Road to Rembetika: Music of a Greek Sub-culture, Songs of Love, Sorrow and Hashish* (Limni, Greece: Harvey & Co., 1975).

[7] See, Viktor Misiano, introduction to *Nikolay Karabinovych: One Place After Another*, available at https://thehumancondition.mmoma.ru/karabinovychnikolay.

[8] W. E. Booth Taylor, foreword, *The Prophetic Word* (London: Carey Press, n.d. [ca. 1946]), p. 7.

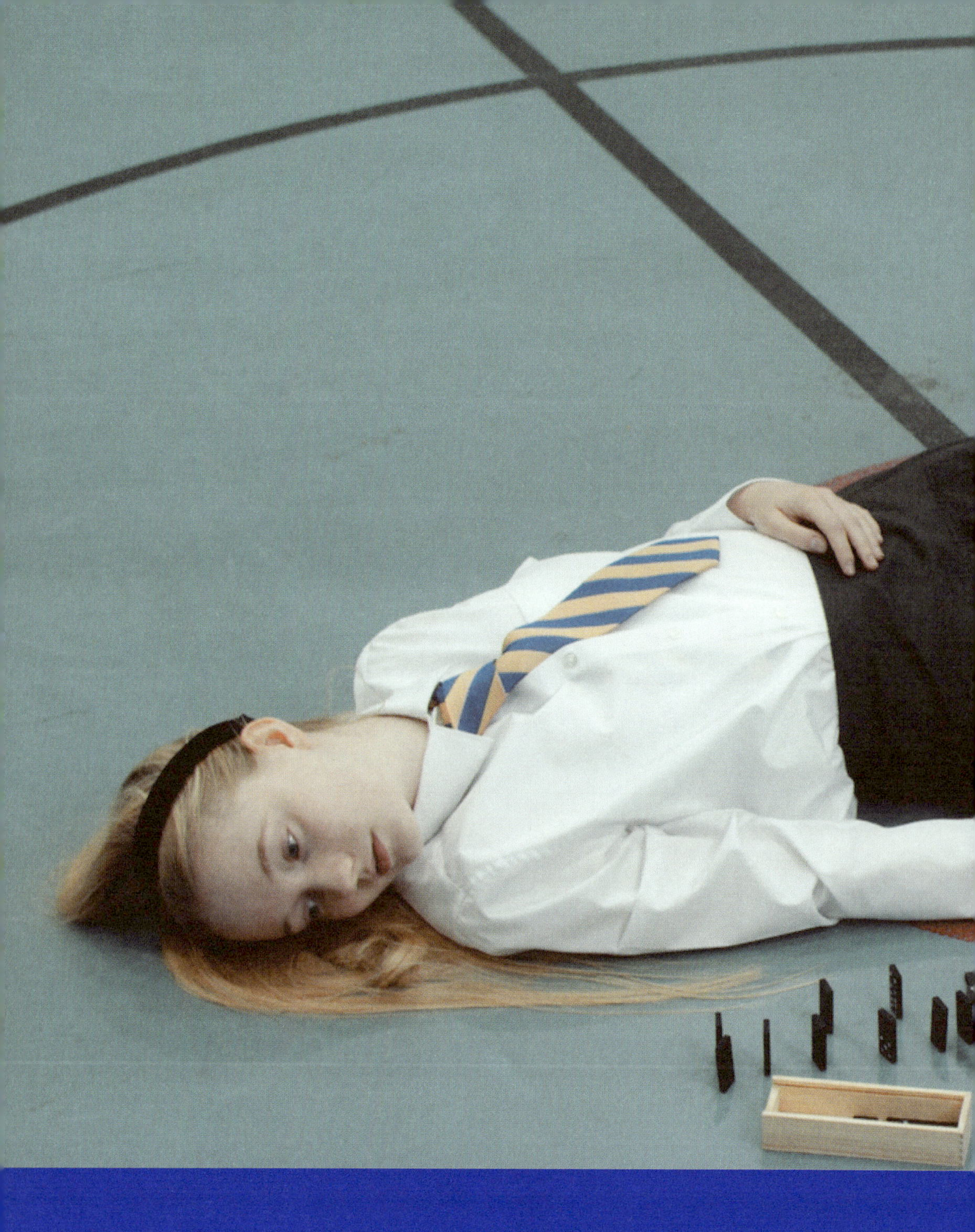

Helen Anna Flanagan, *Gestures of Collapse*, 2019, video still

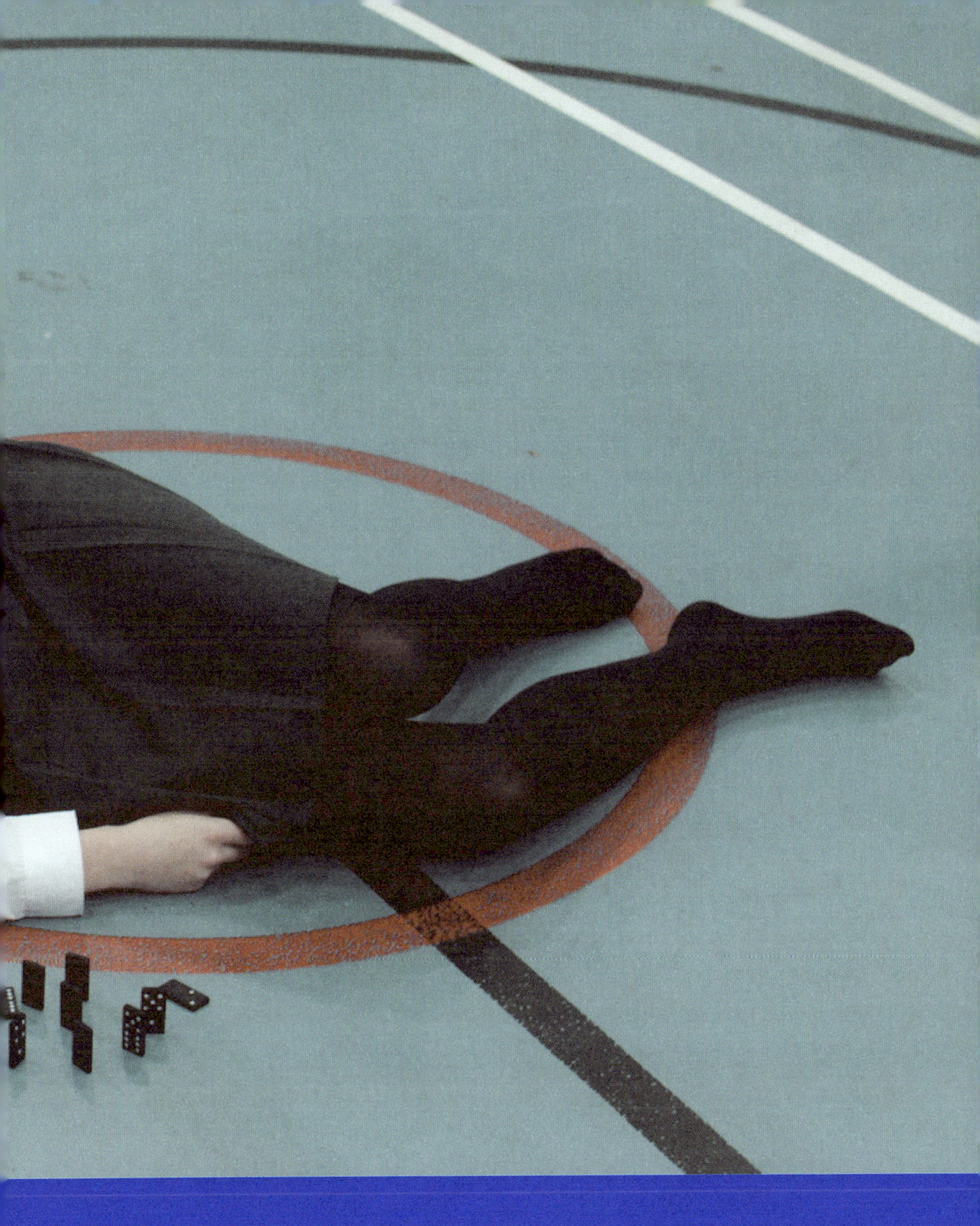

John C. Welchman (2025): This essay discussing an artist book and multipart media work by British, Rotterdam-based artist Helen Anna Flanagan was written for the catalogue of the exhibition of work by HISK participants, In a Long Blink of an Eye curated by Daniella Géo at the Art Deco Gosset building on Rue Gabrielle Petit, Brussels (December 17, 2020 to January 31, 2021). The other artists in the show were: Hanane El Farissi, Katya Ev, Nikolay Karabinovych, Che-Yu Hsu, Diego Lama, Štefan Papčo, Oussama Tabti, Luca Vanello, and Shirley Villavicencio Pizango. Flanagan was awarded the 2019 IKOB Feminist Art Prize which led in 2021 to her first institutional solo exhibition, Gesticulating Wildly, at IKOB – Museum of Contemporary Art, Eupen (May 11 to August 5, 2021) which featured the video- and installation-based Gestures trilogy (2019-20).

One of Helen Flanagan's central interests is in the recursive structures that arise from material and generic spillovers emerging from the collision or overlay of different formats and protocols of making, delivery, and reception. This results not in a metadiscourse organized around certain privileged items–video distributed by projection or monitors, or an installation understood as a coordinated sequence of sculpture-like objects–but in an altogether different mode of abstracting. Various elements associated with the regimen of the filmic, for example, might be discharged from their integrated functionalities and released into narratively disjunctive but otherwise parallel orders of relation. In this way, various quotients of materialization, color, or the formal consolidation of built space (the 'architectural') become gathering points–or invisible armatures–for the exploration of value-intensive regimes of signification that are context-dependent but at the same time reconstituted as zones or through-lines of both affect and social symbolization. This striving for a kind of recharged experiential partitioning calls into question not only what Flanagan refers to as the 'standardized screening format' of moving image media but also the formal constitution of the artwork.[2]

The method and wider implications of this reset are clearest, perhaps, not in Flanagan's work in performance-inflected media, but in a recent project for an artist book, *Billy's Boots*. The organization of the book is configured as an assemblage of layers, each of which has its own logic and interpositional axis through

Exhibitions of Mediality: Helen Anna Flanagan [1]

the book's sequence, but at the same time connects situationally with the other modes of appearance. The most 'recessive' layer is a kind of wallpaper made up of part-elements appropriated from children's join-the-dots diagram-drawings of flies, so that we encounter a shifting sequence of common fly part-objects and unconnected numbers from beginning to end. Secondly, there is a sequence of writings (numbered 1–36), often haiku-like in length, characterized by a mix of description, reflection, dialogue, and action—the whole resembling a freeform film script but shorn of its normal connective tissue. A third layer is comprised of black-and-white 'street photographs' taken by the artist in various parts of the United Kingdom over the course of several years, some showing male figures walking, standing, or sitting in ordinary urban environments, others featuring street-side locations (an alley, a backyard, and several more abstract, peopleless composi-tions and close-ups) or objects (a swing, part of a wrecked car, gas holders). Finally, Flanagan has apportioned doses of green (in a manner that now resembles the *infill* of a child's coloring book—and thus consorts with the dotted fly drawings) across all three elements. A few words are italicized in green, including the title and final words—'My whole damn life!' (though not the quotation marks); and around half of the photos are wholly or partly greened.

The selective greening process in *Billy's Boots* exemplifies Flanagan's method of layering and abstracting, so that the appli-cation of the color infiltrates the other structural layers of the book following a range of richly interleaved protocols. While writ-ten text is turned green in several places (more precisely at the beginning, middle, and end), the first instance of greening within the photographic register of the project occurs in the form of a green inscription that personalizes a beat-up ice-cream van parked at a jaunty angle in the driveway of a semi-detached house: 'Bil-ly's Ices' (we are not sure at first whether this name was a prop-erty of the photograph and thus found in situ, or whether it might have been added in by the artist; but it is, in fact, the former). The remaining additions of green are staged in a telling variety of formats. Some photographs are 'tinted' various shades of green in whole or in part; in a sequence of three photos a single wal-king figure is greened over; in a couple of photographs the line-dividers and curb-adjacent road markings, normally white and yel-low, respectively, are shaded green; in a couple of others, pools, puddles, or water stains are given a limpid green inflection; in one photo the number '4' on the back of a Steven Gerrard (the iconic attacking midfielder who played for Liverpool Football Club and England) jersey goes green; on another, part of a London tube train interior is greened over; and, in a re-chromatizing close-up, the reversed Nike swoosh on the outfit of one of two young men pictured in front of a concrete slab also turns green. The three remaining instances are rather like exceptions that prove the rule. In one case, a photograph of a small, fenced yard set with flower pots, a wheelbarrow, and garden podia features an ornamental display in which the botanical elements (literally–and somewhat congruently) go green; in the last act of colorization in the book, one sneaker sole on a young boy who is being carried across a road by a mostly unseen protagonist is filled in with light green; while the most haunting, and seemingly symbolic, example is the image posted at the center of *Billy's Boots*. Here a metal column, probably a bollard, has been pasted with the image of a young girl with a large bow in her hair and Mickey Mouse ears, holding her hands to her face and wearing an expression we take as fear or consternation–its anxiety redoubled by the added green coloration of her eyes.

Aligning indexical references to the chlorophyll-inflected outcome of photosynthesis or the turquoise and viridian hues of turbulent and stagnant water with intimations of goo and slime, reptilian scales or a generalized toxicity, the green line threaded through Flanagan's book offers a spectrum of chromatic license by pressing home its standard deviation. Thus, green effectively refers to things that become it, but also functions as an ambience or an emblem. In a work that sets out to question the modes of behavior and becoming of the adolescent males picked out page-by-page, it makes good on–and troubles–the elision between toxic and stereotypical masculinity by standing for something as yet unlearned, or in development: the green of immaturity. Stuck on the bottom of a sole it is something picked up and added on in a thin, flattened dose–like a film. Infesting the eyes, it emerges as a body-borne temperament–on the one hand a cypher for bilious irritability; on the other an obsessional envy, what Shakespeare referred to as the 'green sickness' or the 'green-eyed monster.'[3]

How these usages might stack up and their implications be dispensed already presents the need for complex assessment; but this is redoubled when crossed with the metaphorical capacity of other parts of Flanagan's formatting logic. Reflecting on her upcoming exhibition, *Gesticulating Wildly* (2021), she notes, for example, that 'the figure of the fly . . . is a reoccurring motif. . . . The fly references "the fly on the wall" documentary genre from 1970s Britain, a documentary strategy that captured "real" behavior by allowing the camera to continuously run, not unlike current-day reality TV programs.'[4] In this light, the partially formed flies that buzz around *Billy's Boots* stand for behaviors that aren't completely captured or rendered, for routines that are interrupted, or for a mode of documentation that is, by default, incomplete–quite the opposite of the earlier appearance of Dipteran figural language in the art world when the critic Champfleury referred, in the context of a discussion of Gustave Courbet, to 'the flyspeck school of [Jean-Louis Ernest] Meisonnier,' a manner of slavishly exact pictorial realism associated with certain Salon and historical painters in the mid-nineteenth century.[5]

The layering, sequencing, and ghostly interleaving that characterizes *Billy's Boots* looks onto Flanagan's attempt in her performance-inflected film and video work–but especially in the breakouts she stages from media formed as installations– to 'involve different abstracted elements . . . materials, color, architecture, etc.' This concern turns, above all else, on the carefully calibrated attention she vests in activations and transactions spawned by gesture. The artist understands the dispositions of gesture in two key dimensions: as a surplus spun off from the corporeal surfaces of everyday actions; and as a manner super-added, synthetically, to events and exchanges that are more or less preordained or unfurl in a script-like order. Her Gesture Trilogy draws this dialectic alongside three (temporarily) dominant modes of enunciation: one thought through and around particular material substrates (*Gestures of Matter*, 2020); another by way of bodies conceived as structures (*Gestures of Anatomy*, 2019); and the third in relation to a fateful collusion with entropic mimicry (*Gestures of Collapse*, 2019).

Clearly, then, the structural contingencies we encounter so immediately in *Billy's Boots* are also present in the videos. But they are beholden in this significant body of work to a spectrum of refractive dispensations organized by the ways in which gesture is mobilized: in the inflection of bodies and their itineraries; through symbolic objects and their arrays; and by way of language, accent, and intonation–each 'episode' in the trilogy highlighting the emphasis signaled in its title. To this weave of incidents, Flanagan adds two further dispensations: one is aligned with the technical parameters of video production; the other unfolds from one emblematic location abetted by a singular gestural formation associated with each video. So far as the first principle is concerned, the artist emphasizes the orchestration of the scripting process in a matrix of notations that includes movement and exchange; characterological development and interaction; the rhythm and tempo of the camera work and the episodic flow and sequence of the 'action'; as well as the articulation of expression. Each installment of the trilogy is also furnished with what we can term a location assemblage, a dominant, qua-si-architectural or spatial envelope that 'sets' the episode.

In *Gestures of Collapse* this is a gymnasium or sports hall complete with court markings specific to various ball-games–a regulatory system that infiltrates, associatively, or at any rate implicates as code-governed, the behaviors of the young women we encounter. The battery of washing-machines lining the interior of the launderette in which *Gestures of Anatomy* is set is also marked as a system-oriented array defined by repetitive, functional cycles of wash, rinse, and dry. Here the modus operandi of the washing cycle is amplified and allegorized so that it comes into contact with larger cycles of life, including basic bodily functions such as ingestion and excretion; exercise and rest; ovulation and menstruation. Set in a fast-food restaurant, *Gestures of Matter* takes up with the elemental, almost unconscious, rituals transacted in this space–delivered in a rote serialization of movements: reviewing a menu of options; ordering; paying; waiting; and taking (out).

Finally, each of the three videos of the trilogy foreground one gesture that acts as an allegorical subtext, 'pointing' or consolidating them by way of a signature bodily idiom.

In *Gestures of Collapse*, the news reporter prods one of the female performers with his foot while she is on the ground. This poke or kick immediately establishes a set of power and gendered relations, establishing 'authority,' hierarchy, and domination–which, of course, can be mapped back onto the 'news' that the reporter delivers, represents, or *casts*. It also stands for a measure of relational incontinence, as the reporter is immediately associated with a lack of respect and empathy, the effects of which are both underscored and mitigated by the vein of almost caricatural exaggeration that mediates these actions, pointing to a character who is as much ungainly and vulgar as he is exploitative or abusive. But where, the poke seems to demand, is the border between these perceptions? And what is at stake if we accuse or exonerate in pre-set terms? Thinking comparatively, *Gestures of Collapse* seems to turn the premises of Samuel Beckett's *Act Without Words II* (written, in French, in the late 1950s) inside out. Beckett's mime play features two actors, each inside a sack, who are poked by a pole or 'goad' in order to prompt their emergence and routines; Flanagan's video, for its part, begins in the open, its protagonists disgorged, and delivers the motivating act of being poked as the outcome of a different inevitability. To Beckett's wordless intimation of an existential performance goaded on by the unforeseen jabs of fate, *Gestures of Collapse* offers a retort that stages the poke as an emblem of the mirage of mediated representation.

In *Gestures of Anatomy*, the accented gesture is an act of bodily regulation performed by a middle-aged sex worker cutting her toenails. In contrast to the demonstrative, other-directed kicks and pokes of the reporter, the action here is a self-applied moment of personal grooming, normally conducted in private. Its 'exposure' on camera is already supplied with a measure of mild taboo, which Flanagan amplifies and resituates in relation to the character's earlier meditations on the folds and enclosures of her body, its cavities, crevasses, cleavage, and fissures. The caricature implied in *Gestures of Collapse* is answered here by intimations of the grotesque and the abject activated by the visibility and vocalization of corporeal appearance and function–in this case as a measure of becoming in public, in which mundane function and unvarnished appearance add up to something beyond themselves.

The reflex and regulation of the poke and the cut are confronted
by a different–more composite–order of gesture in the third element
of Flanagan's trilogy. *Gestures of Matter* features an older woman
who wields chopsticks not in order to consume a meal but instead to
twist and tweezer the skin on her face in acts of pushing and pull-
ing her eyelids, earlobes, and lips. The invasion of the poke and
subtraction of the cut are met here by a gesture of deliberative
contortion and exposure–which is also, of course, a pantomimic lite-
ralization of caricatural distortion–and offers another grotesque-
rie. As with her other emblematic gestures, the face-pulling in
Gestures of Matter looks onto a related matrix of concerns centering
on the body as an envelope of meat and the purport of carnivorous
consumption, underlined by what the artist describes as the
'Frankenstein' appearance of a mound of gizzards and entrails in
the form of a rotating kebab-like mound.

The stakes of this intricate structure can be better glimpsed if we
open up one of the many implications of the spatial and characterological declensions of *Gestures of Matter*: the idea of the 'line'
itself. Commensurate with the management of post-Enlightenment social order, the line or queue signals general acquiescence to the
'properly' ordered filtration of public or commercial space based on
two social proprieties predicated on a seemingly different logic
of singularity. Lines are formed in accordance with an order of
arrival ('first come, first served') and allow a particular entry,
admission or service on the basis of 'one at a time.' The line thus
harvests a geometric filament of singularities from a plurality of
bodies coming together as a disaggregated mass or a mob; and it
governs virtually every aspect of modern social behavior, from
transit and consumption to sports and leisure. Further, the line
stands in for efficiency, repetition, prohibition, and selection by
way of its function in different sectors: the production line; the
chorus line; the police line or cordon; the criminological line-up;
or the assistant referees in football [soccer], referred to until
the mid-1990s as 'linesmen.' Even the general variegation of commo-
dities and their alignment into groups is signaled by the consort
of things in the capitalist order into product lines.

Flanagan comes at this key figure of social and economic consolidation by examining what lines might do by way of their self-consti-
tution or actions (for example, the passing of sounds), referring to
the effects of a 'transactional line' in order to think through–but
also to disrupt by means of accents of absurdity and dysfunction–

the construct of the line as a preface to consumption. She also thinks through the role of the line as a mimetic figure–a manner of assisted social self-organization that takes specific and generally similar forms. For lines represent the canalization of desire in a precisely figured format: they have become the very patterns of regimented behavior, in which clamor is reduced to articulation; exchange is conditioned by sanctioned outlets; and, in the terms of Georges Bataille, all forms of excretory release are replaced by appropriation and incorporation. Thought in these terms, the line becomes a model of social organization that underwrites a mimetic reflex; based on a subconscious call to order, it is a pronouncement of the preordained that gives onto an understanding of social space itself as an elaborate construct–a location, as Flanagan puts it, that is 'symbolic, coded and loaded.'

1. Giorgio Agamben correlates gesture, as 'pure praxis,' with the sphere of ethics, noting that the 'gesture is the exhibition of a mediality, it is the process of making a means visible as such.' See *Means Without End: Notes on Politics*, trans. Vincenzo Binetti and Cesare Casarino (Minneapolis: University of Minnesota Press, 2000 [1996]), pp. 79, 58.

2. Helen Flanagan, email to the author, May 14, 2020. Unless otherwise indicated, all quotations from the artist are from this exchange.

3. Shakespeare used the term 'green sickness' several times: *Romeo and Juliet*, Act III, Scene v; *Anthony and Cleopatra*, Act III, Scene ii; for 'green-eyed monster' see, *Othello*, Act III, Scene iii.

4. Helen Flanagan, statement on *Gesticulating Wildly*, her one-person exhibition at IKOB - Museum of Contemporary Art, Eupen, Belgium (2021).

5. Champfleury, pseudonym of Jules-François-Félix Husson, *Grandes Figures d'Hier et d'Aujourd'hui: Balzac, Gérard de Nerval, Wagner, Courbet* (Paris: Poulet-Malassis et de Broise, 1861); trans. in Joshua C. Taylor, ed., *Nineteenth-Century Theories of Art* (Berkeley: University of California Press, 1987), p. 328.

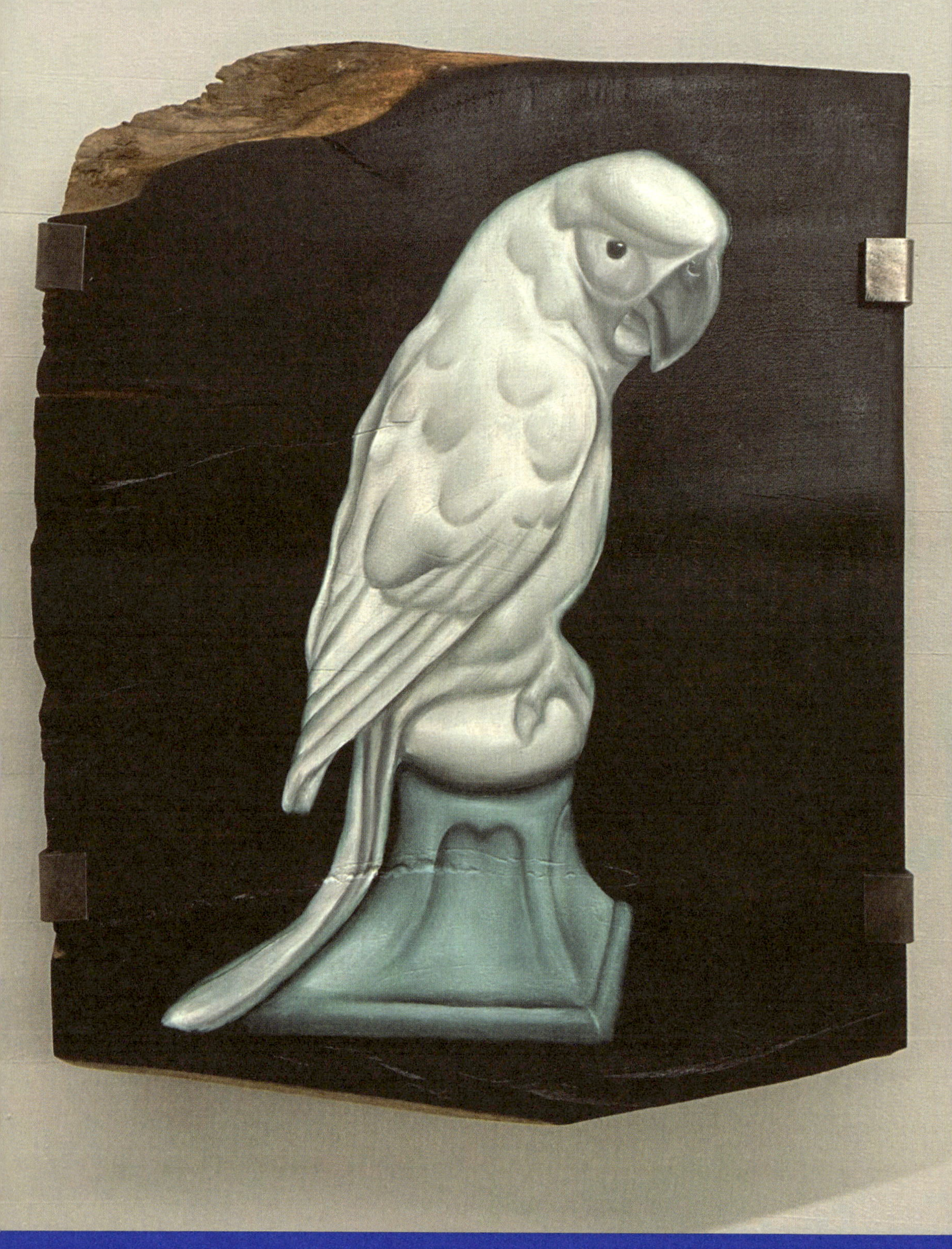

Nelleke Cloosterman, two artworks of five from from *Ara*, installation, 2023, HISK.
Photo: Dani Gherca (©,)

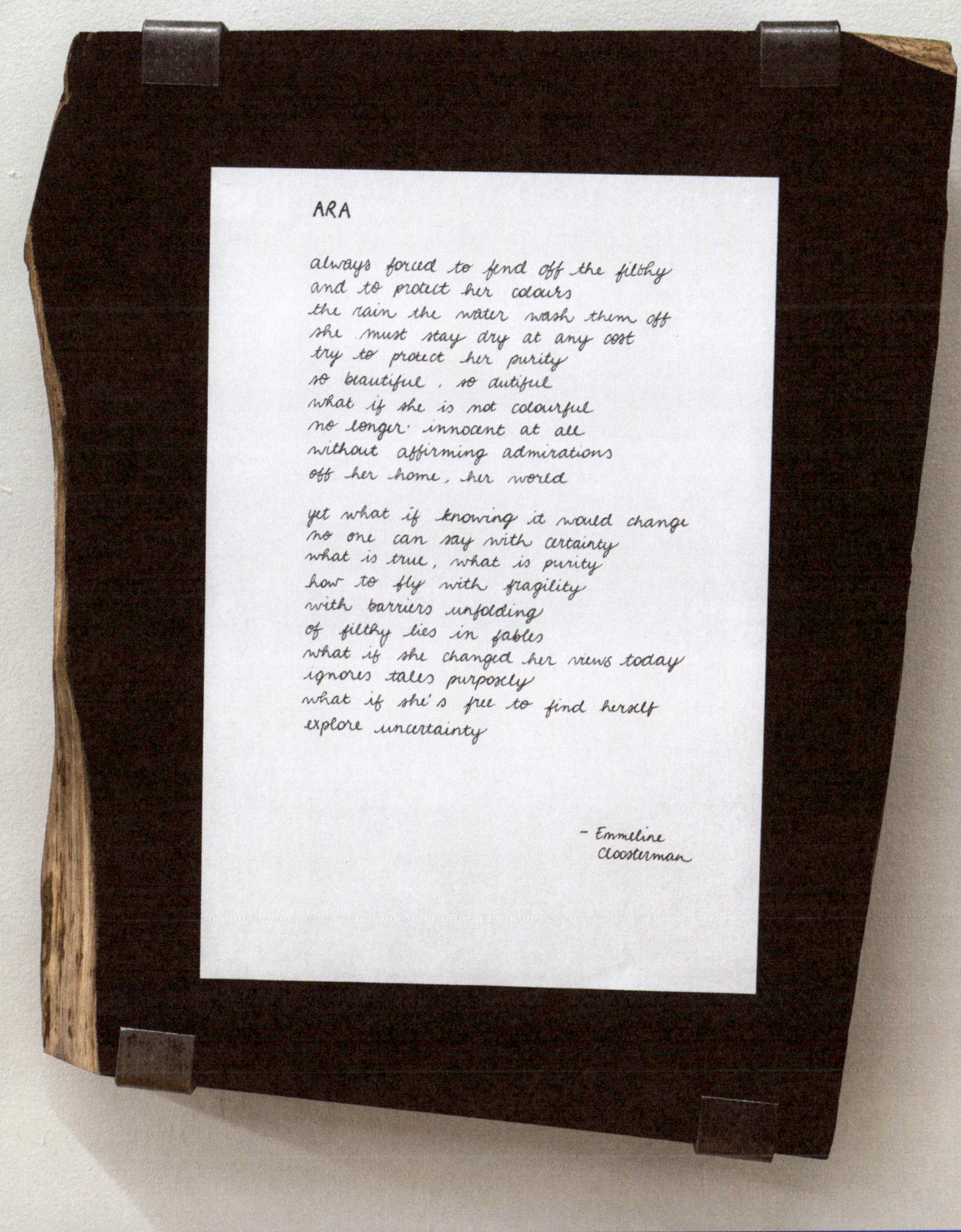

ARA

always forced to fend off the filthy
and to protect her colours
the rain the water wash them off
she must stay dry at any cost
try to protect her purity
so beautiful, so dutiful
what if she is not colourful
no longer innocent at all
without affirming admirations
off her home, her world

yet what if knowing it would change
no one can say with certainty
what is true, what is purity
how to fly with fragility
with barriers unfolding
of filthy lies in fables
what if she changed her views today
ignores tales purposely
what if she's free to find herself
explore uncertainty

- Emmeline
Cloosterman

John C. Welchman (2025): *This essay was written for the cata-logue of the exhibition of work by HISK participants, Various Positions, curated by Sam Steverlynck in the Gosset building on Rue Gabrielle Petit, Brussels (December 9, 2021, to January 30, 2022). The other artists in the show were: Nokukhanya Langa, Hadassa Ngamba, Elisa Pinto, Dani Ghercă, Dries Boutsen, Olivia Hernaïz, Gaëlle Leenhardt, Karel Koplimets, Paulius Šliaupa, and Sandrine Morgante. In a recent exchange Cloosterman notes that she was one of the youngest artists at HISK, admitted when she was twenty-three years old, and re-flects quite candidly on her experience in the program. Not only was she somewhat overwhelmed by the visiting routines, but it was difficult to come to terms with the family and re-ligious contexts, sometimes 'traumatic,' that deeply informed her practice, includingthe work discussed here: 'I even remem-ber asking you not to include anything too personal in the essay.' As a kind of compensation for what couldn't be more directly articulated the artist 'collected . . . images and symbols from art history as a way to work with my story with-out actually speaking about it.'*

Nelleke Cloosterman (2025): *I'm not upset about that decision. I still believe it's important for viewers to connect with the work through their own experiences. It planted the seed for how I work today. I still work with symbolism, because I like contributing to art history in that way, but it's just not a tool anymore [that allows me] not to speak about what it's ac-tually about. Even though the Brussels exhibition marked the end of my time at HISK, it truly feels like the beginning of my journey as an artist in my own right.*

Nelleke Cloosterman's installation of paintings for the 2021 HISK exhibition *Various Positions* is situated in an environment, hand-crafted in wood, that creates a gentle curve, as if the images presented on and within it were part of a distinct cosmos or what the artist refers to as a 'separate world.'[1] The concave hollow of the framing context fosters an atmosphere in which the role of the spectator can be folded into the bearing of a protagonist, thus effacing the separation between object and subject, viewer and

A New Monument to Parrots: Do I Hear a Happy Song?:

Nelleke Cloosterman

participant. At the same time, the artist's 'globalism'—if we can put it like this—is aligned with the conjuring of a spiritual dimension that also underscores, and is possibly predicated on, what recent research in physics has termed a 'world line'—a special type of curve in spacetime.[2] This spatial disposition is reinforced at the level of material and ambience by the spectrum of hues mixed from some forty colors (from greenish white to black) that make up a subtle gradient of tones painted on the inner surface of the parabolic support. Cloosterman thus takes her place in a loose but persistent counter-genealogy that stands up to the deprecation leveled at curvature—by the Cubists, or differently, by Piet Mondrian: those who, as Amédée Ozenfant put in 1916, 'renounce[ed] the charm of living curves.'[3]

Cloosterman's curved expanse provides a location for four constituent elements, along with a marking disposition of colored dots that is developed across and between them: near the center of the curved expanse are two large paintings, one of parrots in a tree, with some of the branches and birds left unfinished; and the other with a concentration of colored, dot-like shapes along with silvery, elongated capsule-like forms, representing, according to the artist's iconographic scheme, bubbles and falling feathers, along with three playing cards. Flanking these works are a painting of a porcelain parrot on a found wooden support—left over from another project by a HISK artist—secured by metal brackets; and a small 'color field' painting, which works like a window or portal and is based on a poem written by one of the artist's sisters, Emmeline, that makes up the final part of the ensemble. In addition to the distribution across the curved surface of the painted colored bubbles, there are other modes of continuity and reciprocity between the parts, including the painted parrots in the tree and on the found wooden fragment, which derive from the same source—an antique parrot-form porcelain that the artist found for sale on an auction website, marked for the German maker Grafenthal with an indication dating its production to between 1906 and 1935. These modes of exchange extend beyond what is literally visible in the installation, for the unseen underside of the auctioned parrot has an impressed eagle, redoubling and compounding the modes of avian reference.

The spaces between the parts of the installation are animated by a dense field of symbological reference organized around the signifying resonance of its central emblems: the parrot (and its feathers) and the bubbles (and their reflected colors). Long present in Cloosterman's work and thinking, the bubbles are emissaries most immediately, from the Vanitas tradition, standing in for frailty, transience, and ephemerality and looking onto the inevitability and possible suddenness of death—part of a seventeenth-century representational program bookended by and reformulated in Jean Siméon Chardin's *Soap Bubbles* (1733–34). But the artist's cascading bubbles are also fragile, shapeshifting, lens-like icons in which the colors and contours of the environment through which they float are present as aura-like refractions. The transmutation between inside and ouside, object and context, aligns with the operating system of the work, but also precipitates specific coloristic emanations—above all in the projective space between the white porcelain parrot (object and painting) and the bubble-caught projection of bright reds, greens, and other hues associated with the plumage of a living bird. Like the otherworldly vivacity of the curving environment in which the elements are situated—or the unseen eagle—the refractive inference presented by the drifting bubbles produces a salient twist in the spacetime continuum, an offstage bend that brings a set of non-declarative premises briefly into view. It is as if the cosmos of the installation flickered without the obvious presence of a light source, or, as the artist puts it, viewers are enabled to 'image what is outside the image.'

The Grafenthal parrot, its painted representations, and the bubble-encased colors that orbit around them by implication face onto another iconographic horizon to which we can ascribe several semantic shifts in the transition between the Middle Ages and modern times. Earlier appearances of parrots in art and literature largely correlate with the symbolism of purity and virginity, as in Jan Van Eyck's *Madonna with the Canon van der Paele* (1436). This association was amplified and reinforced by the strict religious upbringing of Cloosterman and her four sisters, who 'were raised with the idea that our virginity is not ours, but . . . God's to give away.' Some of the deficits prompted by the sacrifice of this constraint appear in recurring images—manifest elsewhere in Cloosterman's work—of wingless birds, for which, in turn, the detached feathers in the current installation are a cipher. Clearly, the white porcelain parrot offers a reprise of the constraints and reduction of virginity, which are, in turn, challenged and abandoned by the act of representation and further exploded by the color-affirming orbit of the bubbles. One scholar notes that the shift to the characteristically modern symbolic field of the parrot, exemplified in '[Ben] Jonson's *Volpone*, which memorably embodies the topos of mindless, psittacine repetition in the character of Sir Politic Would-Be,' was, in fact, ushered in and abetted by the Reformation—in that parrots, which had for some generations been associated with Papal wealth and prestige, were now subject to the withering

Protestant critique of Catholic and pontifical ostentation, pomp, overelaboration, and mindless mimicry, the outer reaches of which informed the puritanical order to which Cloosterman (whose very name derives, by happenstance, from cloistered retreat) was subject.[4]

The release at stake here is quite something. It's not just that the parrot, as Edouard Manet, Gustave Courbet, and other nineteenth-century artists attested, becomes the faithful, if still ultra-mimetic, companion of various painted women. More dramatically, the porcelain parrot is the guardian a new round of secrets, convened in its own period specificity in the 1920s. For this is when the parrot was fired up into a remarkable afterlife. Francis Picabia inveighs against the 'ponderous and half-witted sentiment of morality [that] rules the entire world' but especially religious thinking: 'The moralists,' he wrote in 1923, 'never discern the moral facts of appearances, the Church for them is a morality like the morality of drinking water, or of not daring to wash one's ass in front of a parrot! All that is arbitrary.'[5] Half a decade later, Salvador Dalí presciently transforms Cloosterman's roving spots into speech bubbles ventriloquizing the prismatic abandon to which they point: 'The tiny parasols in all the colors in the world on which one could make out precious trichromatic prints depicting various types of parrots and many species of animals in a state of rut on whose backs were paint-ed famous lakes and other kinds of twilights.' Elsewhere in the same early text, the bubble is re-drawn as a token of the biological form-lessness represented by mucous spreading around the radius of Dalí's dissident globe: 'There is a mucus standing up at the edge of a curb-stone. And another mucus, standing up on my fingertip, ready to fly away. And another mucus, upright 20 meters away, on a stone that looks like a monument to parrots. And another mucus, calm on a moth fourty meters away, that is a happy song...[6]

[1]. All quotations from the artist are from discussions and an email exchange in October and November 2021.

[2]. See for example, F. Reese Harvey's discussion of Special Relativity in 'Euclidean / Lorentzian Vector Spaces,' in *Spinors and Calibrations* (Cambridge, MA.: Academic Press, 1990), pp. 62-67.

[3]. Amédée Ozenfant, 'Notes on Cubism' (1916); trans. in Charles Harrsion and Paul Wood, ed., *Art in Theory 1900-1990: An Anthology of Changing Ideas* (Oxford: Blackwell, 2003), p. 227.

[4]. Bruce Thomas Boehrer, 'The Cardinal's Parrot Book,' chapter 2 of *Animal Characters Book: Nonhuman Beings in Early Modern Literature* (Philadelphia: University Pennsylvania Press, 2010), p. 103; Stable URL: https://www.jstor.org/stable/j.ctt3fj3qO.5.

[5]. Francis Picabia, 'Thank you, Francis!' [Francis Merci!] in *Littérature*, n.s. no. 8 (January 1, 1923), pp. 16 - 17; trans. in Lucy Lippard, ed., *Dadas on Art* (Englewood Cliffs, NJ: Prentice-Hall, 1971); reprinted in *Art in Theory 1900 - 1990*, p. 275.

[6]. Salvador Dalí, 'Con el sol' [With the Sun], *La Gaceta Literaria* (Madrid) no. 54, March 15, 1929, p. 1.

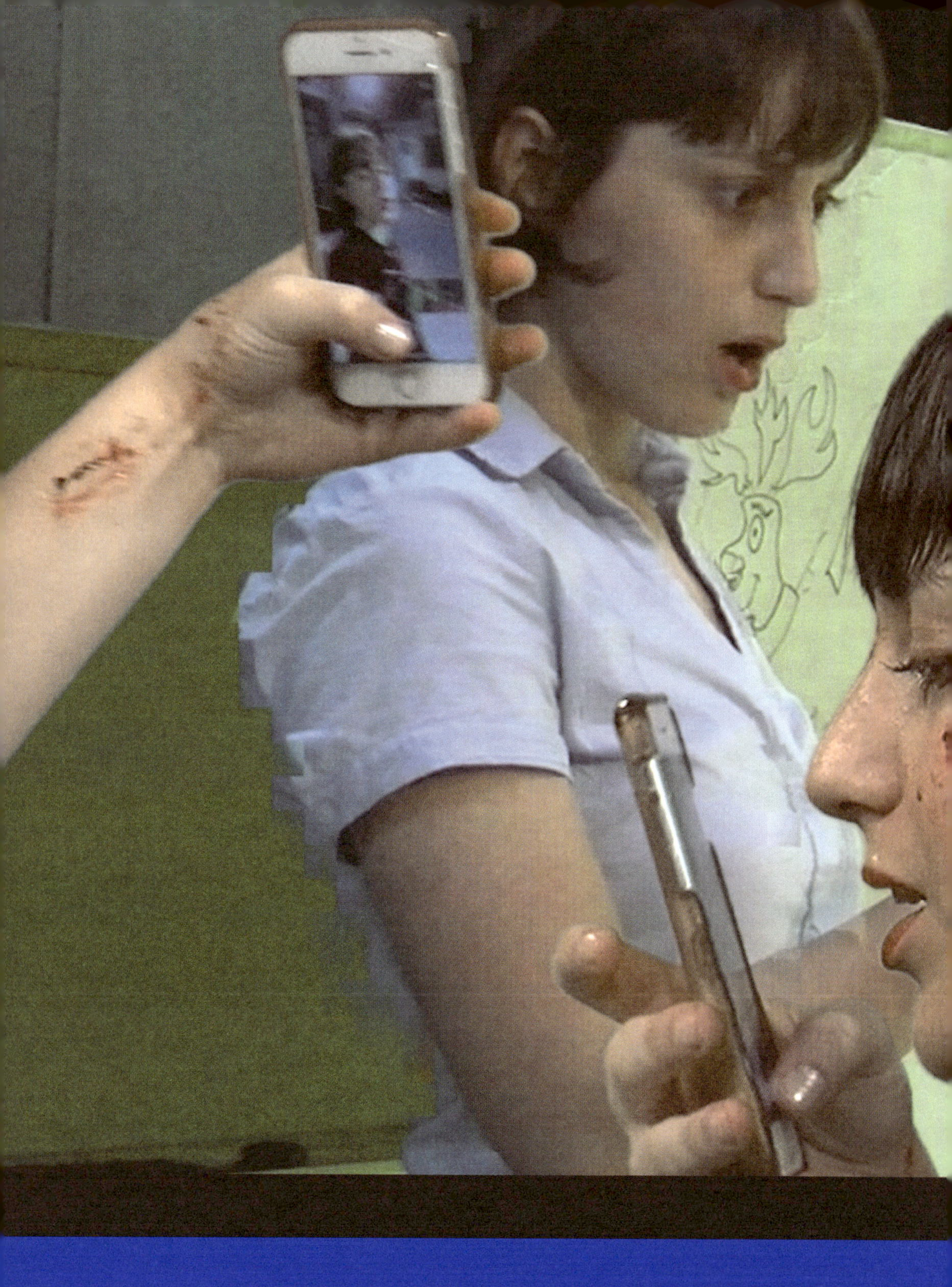

Danielle Kaganov, *Alpha Channel II*, 2023, film and performance, 17 min.

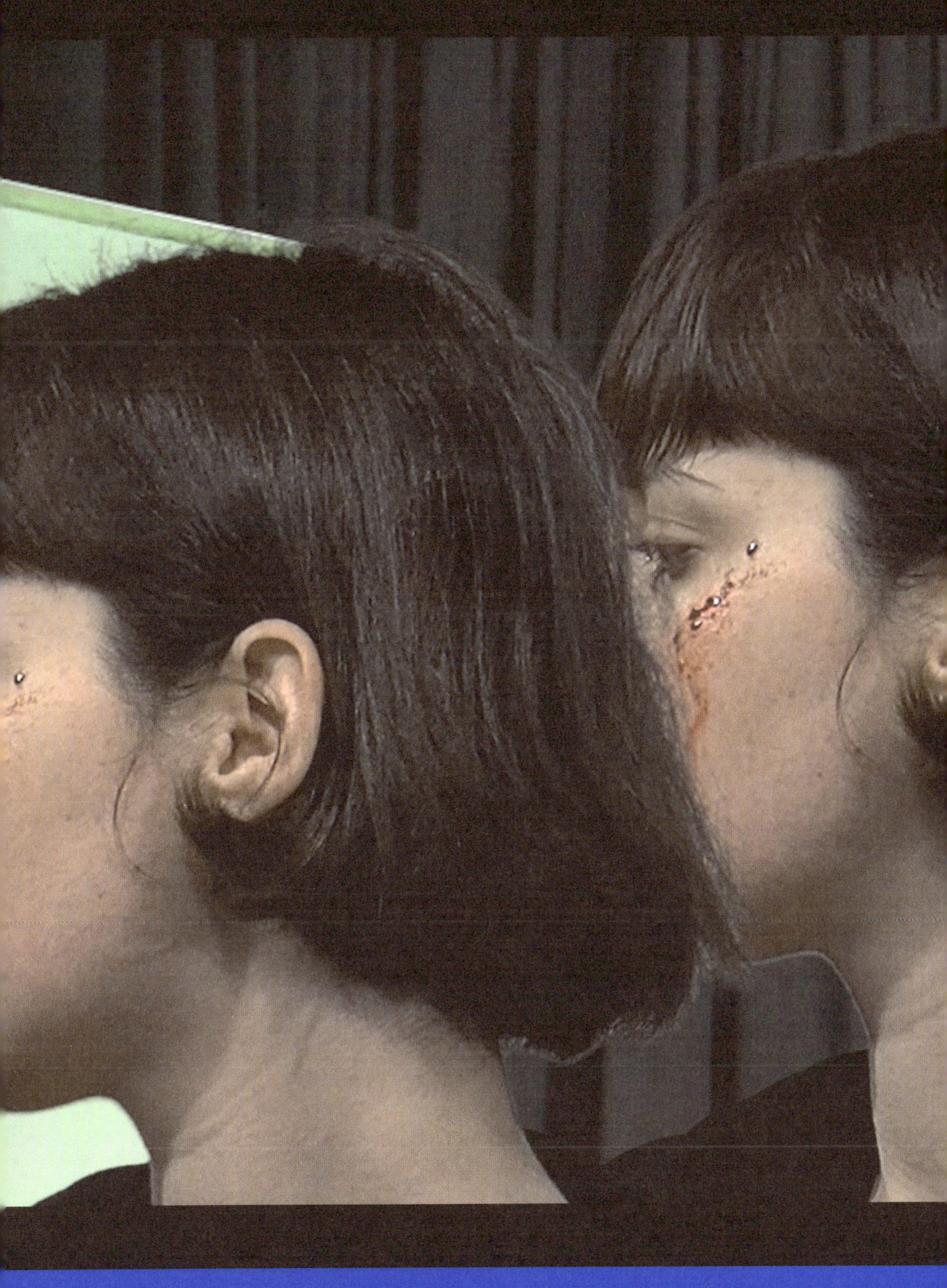

John C. Welchman (2025): *This essay on a performance and film work by Israeli-Russian multidisciplinary artist Danielle Kaganov was written for the catalogue of the exhibition of work by HISK participants,* Staying in the Gap *curated by Yue Yuan at the Société d'Electricité, Brussels (January 20, to February 5, 2023). The other artists in the show were: Fabiola Burgos Labra, Jim Campers, Hamed Dehqan, Maëlle Dufour, Maud Gourdon, Axel Korban, Axelle Lenaerts, Paola Siri Renard, Jivan van der Ende, and Yue Yuan. Kaganov's work, here and elsewhere, raises difficult, challenging, and important issues at the intersection of formations of violence—individual, collective, and political—and projections of fantasy and desire. One of its strengths arrives with the resourceful finesse that pushes these questions through a minefield of possibilities that bears witness to how terror and ecstasy are implicated a technology-assisted centrifuge in which tragedy, irony, and parody are compounded.*

If there is a leading premise that supplies the recent work in media-performance and film of Danielle Kaganov it is that signal aspects of Israeli rightist politics have been organized for more than two decades by an oddball congregation of media managers, producers, and acolytes who are fortified by complicated and explicitly, often crudely, visualized fantasies of violence, sexuality, irony, and submission. Such formations are, self-evidently, antithetical to the implicitly puritanical, pro-family counter-urban-bohemian mantras of other right-leaning regimes, whether in the United States, Russia, Hungary, or elsewhere—encoded in reflex *Blut und Boden* xenophobias layered with scrambled enervations of moral rectitude.[1] One aspect of these more standardized constructions is emblematized by Benjamin 'Bibi' Netanyahu's excruciatingly long, one-take video posts of banal routines in his home and office captured by a fixed cam that precisely relinquish not just the allure of what is elsewhere erotically charged but also the jump-cuts and shifting POVs that animate it. As Kaganov's auteur-cum-documentary-style in person 'voice-over' put it, these streams were 'filmed in a very simple medium shot. He was repeating the same message again and again. It was a classic indoctrination on the one hand, but on the

Over to Annabella: Oral and Other Fantasies (in and out of Power):

Danielle Kaganov

other hand, there was something a bit too exposed about them, and you could see some cracks.'[2]

If the narcissistically tinged rhetorical diminuendo of Netanyahu's video-feeds presents one pole of the right-wing media spectrum in Israeli politics, the other side has been supplied with a language of undeclarative tendentiousness by Senia Waldberg, the 'Russian esoteric geek'[3] who achieved notoriety in the earlier 2000s with his blog 'Holy Senia' and by the even more slippery figure of Srulik (a nickname diminutive of 'Israel'), who worked for Avigdor Lieberman, the leader of Israel Beiteinu, a non-religious far right party and then for Netanyahu, before, like Waldberg, going into advertising and marketing. A would-be denizen of the art and club scenes at the turn of the twenty-first century as well as of the emerging World Wide Web, Srulik took up with performative camouflage dressing up in a burqa in one instance and as DJ Cock in others—donning a yellow, plastic penis-form outfit and joining a gay parade. He thus games with the two putative extremes of corporeal declaration—the religious-inflected 'prudery' of the burqa and the manic prurience of the all-genital self-display; the former got-up to stage a cynically racist, sexually charged misogynistic up-skirt sneak-pic; the later an overt infiltration purposed to compete with and outflank the libidinal theatricality of an LGBTQ+ festival. Srulik's mannered self-consciousness even extended to deflective parodies of anti-right, politically tinged satire when he entered into dialogue with Sascha Baron Cohen's send-up of the 'swollen, testosteronic Israeli pro-gun advocate' Colonel Erran Morad in the 'Kinderguardians' segment that concluded the first episode of his 2018 Showtime series *Who Is America?*[4] Waldberg, we might note, is the PR contact cited by Yahoo.Finance in a notice published on March 13, 2023 about the launch of Annabella, 'the world's first breast pump to simulate a baby's tongue during the pumping process.'[5]

A second condition for *Alpha Channel II* follows on. For this primal scene predicated on a mutant conjunction of the erotically gratuitous and administrative nostalgia is complicated from the outset by Kaganov's self-insinuation as a citizen, voyeur, desiring subject, and, importantly, as a savvy (and sassy) social and new media creator and producer in her own right. Kaganov activates—and simultaneously questions—her own agency by soliciting first (and unsuccessfully) the larger and more formally ordered campaign and PR operations of Netanyahu and then the more informal networks of Lieberman's Israel Beiteinu, a context in which her Jewish-Russian roots played quite centrally to the audience and policy strategies of the Soviet-born politician who served as Minister of Finance between 2021 and 2022 and twice as Deputy Prime Minister of Israel (from 2006 to 2008 and 2009 to 2012).

Kaganov orients herself to this work in a manner that echoes the issue-evacuated political disingenuity of Srulik: 'The way I portray myself in the work,' she noted in a recent conversation, 'is also like this'–for the most part knowingly.[6] The work of the artist is thus founded as a staged misrepresentation within the campaign-like charade of a rightist media imaginary. Part of this address is clearly 'a fantasy space of prurience' (JCW) that emerged when Kaganov first encountered Waldberg's blog as a Tel Aviv teen. But it is formatted as a fantasy-cum-delusion predicated on a knotty weave of fascination and disgust. Never a purely 'sexual fantasy, [it was] more [like] a power [trip]' driven on in one dimension by a bid for imagistic and directorial control and in another by fitfully shared compulsions around the production of and encounter with 'excess' (DK).

A third platform on which *Alpha Channel II* builds is historical, figured around two contiguous blocks of time. The most obvious chronology tracks the some quarter of a century from around 2000 to now, coterminous with the artist's own formation, in which internet-abetted 'new' and 'social' media (and now AI) developed into mass-distributed, omnivorously addictive, consciousness-sculpting forces. In her research and thinking, however, Kaganov reaches back another twenty-five years to around 1975, a moment in which commentary–by Pier Paulo Pasolini, Susan Sontag, Gianfranco Sanguinetti, among others–engages with the 'end of the 1960s,' the depredations of consumer culture, the dominion of neoliberalism, and the ghastly perseverance and reformatting of fascist polity. These discussions are both symptomatic and premonitory.

Attending to the signs of fascist continuity, Sontag, for example, points to the adumbration on the cover of a volume under review on SS regalia (by Jack Pia) of a 'breviary of a sexual fantasy,' predicated on formations of 'innocuousness . . . practicality'[7] that clearly anticipate the more anxious and latently deviant leavening of sexual inertia and political aimlessness in the media declamations of Waldberg and Srulik. Less than a week earlier Pasolini had published his eco-political allegory 'Il vuoto del potere in Italia' (often referred to as 'Where Have All the Fireflies Gone?') in the Italian daily *Corriere della Sera*.[8] Sublimating the sexual allusion fomented in the image of points of light animating the courtship rituals of fireflies–creatures that were disappearing under the inexorable pressures of pollution and suburbanization–Pasolini inveighed against the depredations of consumerism, conformity, and linguistic and other monocultures engendered by the quietly savage continuum that conjoined contemporary Christian-Democrat politics with fascist antecedents. Kaganov has, I think, engaged with the apparent paradox pointed to in one of the most challenging discussions of Pasolini's lament: 'Culture is not what protects us from barbarity and what must be protected from barbarity; culture is the very space in which the new barbarity's intelligent forms flourish.'[9]

[1]. See, Corey Robin, 'Family Values Fascism: From Vichy to Donald Trump,' *Crooked Timber*, August 16, 2015; available at https://crookedtimber.org/2015/08/16/family-values-fascism-from-vichy-to-donald-trump/.

[2]. Danielle Kaganov, script for *Alpha Channel II* (2023), as presented at HISK [Hoger Instituut voor Schone Kunsten/Higher Institute for Fine Art], Brussels, September 18, 2023; unpublished, np.

[3]. Ibid.

[4]. Sophie Gilbert, 'Who Is Sacha Baron Cohen Satirizing?' *The Atlantic*, July 19, 2018; available at https://www.theatlantic.com/entertainment/archive/2018/07/who-is-sacha-baron-cohen-satirizing/565397/.

[5]. See, https://finance.yahoo.com/news/annabella-first-breast-pump-simulate-122700190.html.

[6]. Danielle Kaganov in conversation with John C. Welchman, HISK studio, Brussels, September 19, 2023. Unless otherwise indicated all subsequent quotes from Kaganov (DK) and Welchman (JCW) are from this unpublished discussion.

[7]. Susan Sontag, 'Fascinating Fascism,' in *Under the Sign of Saturn* (New York: Vintage, 1981), p. 100; first published in *New York Review of Books*, vol. XXII, no. I (February 6, 1975).

[8]. Pier Paolo Pasolini, 'Il vuoto del potere in Italia' (The Power Vacuum in Italy) *Corriere della Sera*, February 1, 1975; trans. Ruth Pérez-Chaves, *Comparative Cinema*, vol. VII, no. 12 (2019). The essay was republished in *Scritti corsari* as 'L'articolo delle lucciole.'

[9]. Alain Brossat, 'De l'inconvénient d'être prophète dans un monde cynique et désenchanté,' *Lignes*, vol. 18 (2005): 47-48. Brossat's thought is cited in another useful disquisition on Pasolini's 1975 essay: Georges Didi-Huberman, 'Hells? (On Pier Paolo Pasolini)' in Didi-Huberman, *Survival of the Fireflies* (Minneapolis: University of Minnesota Press, 2018); available at https://my-blackout.com/2022/05/11/georges-didi-huberman-hells-on-pier-paolo-pasolini/.